# Dardevle's Guide to Fishing

Other Books by David Richey

*A Child's Introduction to the Outdoors*
*Steelheading for Everybody*
*Shakespeare Guide to Great Lakes Fishing*
*Getting Hooked on Fishing (with J. Knap)*
*Trout Fisherman's Digest (editor)*
*Sea Run (contributing author)*
*The Small Boat Handbook*
*How to Catch Trophy Freshwater Gamefish*
*The Brown Trout Fisherman's Guide*

All photographs in this book are by David or Kay Richey except as noted.

# Dardevle's Guide to Fishing

## by David Richey

DORRANCE & COMPANY • *Philadelphia and Ardmore, Pa.*

Copyright © 1978 by David Richey
*All Rights Reserved*
ISBN 0-8059-2561-9
Library of Congress Catalog Card Number: 78-67743
Printed in the United States of America

*To my parents, Lawrence and Helen Richey; I'm eternally grateful to them for giving me the opportunity as a child to experience the joys of fishing. Without this initial enthusiasm I may never have come to love the sport as I do now.*

# Contents

| | |
|---|---|
| Introduction | 1 |
| Dardevles Are Great for Panfish | 3 |
| How to Catch Salmon on Dardevles | 10 |
| Types of Retrieves | 21 |
| Tricks That Take Stubborn Fish | 27 |
| Northern Pike and Muskies | 33 |
| A New Look at the Dardevle Klicker | 47 |
| How Dardevles Are Made | 53 |
| Rainbow and Brown Trout Tactics | 54 |
| Lake Trout Are Suckers for Dardevles | 64 |
| The Spinner and the Steelhead | 73 |
| Largemouth and Smallmouth Bass | 79 |
| Walleyes and Sauger Go Nuts for Dardevles | 88 |
| Thin Spoons Get the Fish | 96 |
| Water Temperature | 102 |
| What Color Lure? | 107 |
| How to Hire a Guide | 110 |
| Arctic Char and Grayling | 116 |
| Dardevle Ice Fishing Techniques | 124 |
| Saltwater Fishing: A Dardevle Natural | 129 |
| Exotic Dardevle Trophies | 132 |

## *Getting Hooked*

Dardevles have been around for many years and have hooked as many fishermen as fish. I know of no other lure which has steadfastly maintained such a reputation. It's a proven fact: these lures have no rival when it comes to producing good catches of game fish.

My introduction to Dardevles came during the summer of 1954 when my parents took my brother and me on a pike-fishing expedition to Batchawana Bay, Ontario. Before my folks were firmly ensconced in our temporary quarters I had strung my rod and was casting a small Dardevle into the Batchawana River.

The lure sailed out on the early summer breeze. In my youthful enthusiasm, however, I had failed to note that one didn't fish for big northern pike with six pound mono. The fact that I didn't have a wire leader hadn't crossed my mind.

My casting was flawless, as I remember the incident, and about twenty minutes went by before the weeds parted in front of the dock and a huge set of toothy jaws swept forward and nailed the Dardevle. I set the hook and held on tight as a big pike bored for the middle of the river with his back creasing the water's surface.

I was a young, scrawny kid with few muscles, and that big fish had me working overtime trying to cope with his long runs. I'd let the drag on my early-model spinning reel take line, and I did my best to pressure the pike back when he decided to sulk. This seesaw battle continued for half an hour, until the owner of the lodge sauntered down with a gaff and made a lucky swipe as the big northern cruised past the end of the dock.

I was arm-weary, tired and exuberant at the same time; I couldn't stop talking to my brother and parents about the terrific fight the fish had given me. It was one of the biggest thrills of a thirty-year fishing career. That jumbo pike weighed just over nineteen pounds and represented the thrill of a lifetime for any youngster.

The point behind this anecdote is that similar thrills await any angler willing to give the Dardevle line of lures a thorough testing. These spoons and spinners have proven themselves throughout the world, both with sophisticated, angler-wise fish and with the naive species in bush country. All gamefish have to eat in order to stay alive; and Dardevles, with their unique action and color combinations, appeal to any gamefish, large or small.

Take a youngster fishing. Introduce your children to the sport which will provide a lifetime of pleasure. Teach them to enjoy fishing as a solo pastime—or in the companionship of others.

## Dardevles Are Great for Panfish

Many fishermen believe the only time a Dardevle should be used is when casting weedy shorelines for northern pike. Nothing could be further from the truth.

Although Dardevles come in many sizes, shapes and colors, very few anglers have tried tossing the smaller-sized models at panfish. Within the last few years I've switched from the bulldog scrap of big salmon and trout to the dogged, water-circling battle of bluegills, sunfish, crappies and yellow perch. The challenge of taking large specimens of these fish gives a boost to my ego, and they provide some fine eating.

One good thing about panfish is that they are available to many fishermen on a year-round basis. Spring or fall months find eager schools of bluegills and sunfish hugging shorelines or near any man-made structures such as swimming rafts, docks, sunken boats and the like.

The dead-heat months of summer represent a slowdown for many panfishermen because they usually work the shoreline in much the same manner as during the spring. The bigger fish just aren't there; they've trailed the cooler water down, and many times fish will be found near bottom or off a drop-off, in twenty to thirty feet of water.

One time several years ago I took my daughters to a small lake near home. The lake was noted for big gills, but hot summer weather had forced the fish to take refuge in deeper water.

A local bait dealer had recommended live bait. "Crickets will get them in twenty feet of water," he'd said. He had given us a clue to the whereabouts of the gills, but we didn't buy any bait. We planned to use small Dardevles.

We launched our boat and hooked up my sonar unit as we motored away from shore. We found a shelf which dropped from twelve to twenty feet near the outside edge of a weed bed. The wind was perfect for a slow downwind drift, perfect for our type of deepwater bluegill fishing.

I attached a Dardevle Midget, red with a white stripe, to Kimmy's line, and a smaller silver-colored Skeeter to Stacey's. The girls were instructed to cast parallel to the drop-off and along the outside edge of the weeds. They were told to allow both lures to sink slowly to bottom and then retrieve at a snail's pace. Kimmy's Midget sank much faster, and soon she was inching the lure slowly back along bottom.

The lure was halfway back to the boat when it stopped for an instant. She set the hooks hard enough to barb a tarpon, and far below the boat a platter-sized bluegill began its circling, head-shaking battle.

Stacey began cranking hard to get her lure in and I told her to slow down. I explained that bluegills, the deepwater variety, often school up and that she might find a willing biter. Her reel made two revolutions and then her lure stopped. "I'm snagged up," she hollered. She tugged two or three times trying to free her lure when the line began slanting toward deeper water.

Kimmy's fish, a nine-inch bluegill, was led to the net, where I slid it onto the stringer. Stace fought her pug-nosed bluegill toward the boat, where it cut tiny figure eights in the water until it was tired. I added it to the stringer with Kimmy's, and suddenly the day's fishing had taken on new meaning to the girls.

By the time the sun began sinking in the west with an orange glow, we'd added another half dozen bull bluegills to the stringer as well as a live basket brimful with smaller five- to eight-inch fish.

Slow retrieves are deadly when fishing deep for big panfish. The fish are reluctant to chase a lure far, and bluegills in particular often follow a slow-moving lure much farther before striking than they would a fast-moving spoon.

Jigging is another means of taking lunker bluegills, sunfish and crappies during warm weather. One of the largest redear sunfish I've taken fell to a jigged Midget fished from a drifting boat.

Crappies and yellow perch are suckers for a slow jigging technique. I normally look for crappies along brushy shorelines, although these fish often suspend themselves over deep water. Perch are normally bottom-loving fish, and the angler should begin fishing in deeper water before moving closer to shore.

I'll often anchor directly over a brushpile, tie on a Midget or Skeeter, and jig straight down into the brush. To minimize snagging and loss of lures I'll often remove two of the three hooks with wire cutters. A

*This father-son team casts small Dardevles to spawning bluegills in Florida.*

*This young lady casts a small fly rod-sized Dardevle Skeeter to bluegills in an Illinois farm pond. With her is Leo Pachner, publisher of the famous* Farmpond Harvest *magazine of Kankakee, Illinois.*

slow, up-and-down jigging technique is deadly on crappies and a good method of filling the freezer with tasty fillets.

Slow trolling is a very productive method of taking bull bluegills. I usually use a silver or red-with-white-stripe Midget and a quarter-ounce sinker attached about two feet ahead. Prime locations are around the deepwater edges of weed beds.

Big gills prowl the deepwater edges of weed beds, and a small minnow-imitating lure is just the right size for nice fish. There are times when large schools of big bluegills will frequent the middle of a lake during midday. They often move up from bottom just before dark; early evening hours are prime times to catch big fish.

As effective as small Dardevles are on panfish, I've found it extremely effective on all panfish to add a wee sliver of white pork rind or a small angleworm or red worm to the hooks. Keep the pork rind or worm short to minimize the fish's tendency to merely nip at the lure. I've found a slow, up-and-down movement of the rod tip to be best. This will cause the baited lure to undulate, and big panfish find this an irresistible combination.

When sunfish and bluegills work the spring shorelines, I often wade slowly along with a fly rod and Skeeter. This 1/32-ounce lure casts easily with a long rod and is just the greatest for teasing bulls off spawning beds. Cast the lure on one side of the saucer-shaped spawning bed, allow it to sink and tumble into the bed on a slack line, and many times a protective male will grab the tiny spoon. A slow retrieve will often provoke a strike as the lure wobbles up out of the bed.

Yellow perch are some of the most delightful panfish for eating. They often congregate in large schools, and the Dardevle fisherman with his vast array of lures can often make some mighty fine catches.

I like to fish perch when they are schooling off river mouths in the springtime. The fish are tightly packed, seem to be ravenously hungry, and are easy to catch.

I've found two methods of fishing well suited to perch fishing. I like to take these fish on ultralight spinning tackle. I use either two- or four-pound mono and a silver Dardevle Midget. With this outfit you can cast a country mile. I'll cast off a rivermouth, allow the spoon to flutter down on a tight line, and retrieve just fast enough to bring out the wiggle. Perch often strike anything smaller than themselves, and this method brings out the competitive spirit of feeding perch. I've had three or four strikes on one retrieve. If a retrieve just under the surface doesn't produce, try letting the lure sink a bit longer before beginning the retrieve. It often takes experimentation with sinking times and retrieval speeds to determine which combination is most interesting to the fish.

A technique I've worked out for locating midsummer perch is to begin drifting a windblown course from deep water to shallower depths. I'll usually begin drifting in twenty-five feet of water and work in to about ten feet.

I normally use a silver-colored Midget and lower the spoon to the bottom. As I drift downwind I'll jig the lure up and down rhythmically. Six-inch twitches are sufficient, but keep the spoon flashing and dancing near bottom. Once you catch a nice perch, lower the anchor and continue fishing until the school plays out. Then begin another methodical search until you locate the perch again.

*This nice crappie was taken from Lake Okeechobee in Florida on a Dardevle Midget worked on a cane pole.*

Panfish are found anywhere in North America where lake waters warm sufficiently. Some of the best sunfish, and especially bluegill, fishing is found in southern states, where the fish have a longer growing season. I've made some excellent catches of bluegills from Florida's Lake Okeechobee.

Crappies are common throughout waters east of the Mississippi River, but, again, southern states have some of the best.

Yellow perch hold forth throughout the Great Lakes states and represent one of the most sought-after fish in the area. I'd rate the current perch fishing in lakes Michigan, Huron and Erie as some of the best in the world. Certain inland lakes produce good perch fishing, but the best fishing is in the Great Lakes proper where unlimited forage fish allow perch to grow big, fast.

Panfish are not difficult to take with lures providing the fisherman realizes they have small mouths and fishes with dainty-sized lures and hooks. The smallest varieties of Dardevle are letter-perfect for panfish.

*This young fisherman swings in a nice bluegill taken on a small Dardevle.*

*These two anglers discuss which Dardevle to use for their fishing trip.*

# How to Catch Salmon on Dardevles

Since the advent of coho and chinook plantings in the Great Lakes during the mid-1960s, salmon fishing has taken a decided turn for the better. Fishermen intent on taking these species no longer have to make long treks to the West Coast for action.

There is much to be said for fishing the rich Pacific shoreline anywhere from California north to Alaska; the fish are present in good numbers,

*Trolling for Great Lakes or Pacific salmon often means fishing in a tightly knotted pack of boats similar to this.*

especially in Oregon and Washington. But lakes Michigan and Huron are currently offering a brand of action incomparable to that found anywhere else.

Most salmonids found in Pacific waters are the result of natural reproduction. The Great Lakes, on the other hand, depend almost entirely on hatchery reproduction and plantings of several million coho and chinook yearly; this is the key to top-flight fishing sport in the Midwest.

By and large, salmon fishing is open-water angling during ice-free months. A limited number of salmon are taken yearly by ice fishermen, but the vast majority fall to trollers plying open water.

Trolling is probably the number one method of taking coho and chinook. With a few exceptions, techniques that regularly take coho will

*These anglers caught two silvery coho salmon from fish-rich Lake Michigan near Manistee, Michigan on Jr. Flutter Devles.*

also work on their larger cousins. The following techniques will work anywhere salmon are found, whether in the Great Lakes or the Pacific Ocean.

Spring fishing is both predictable and productive, although the fish, as a rule, are much smaller in size than the adult summer and fall fish. This smallness, incidentally, makes for fine taste, and many fishermen reserve angling time for that period just after the ice goes out to catch salmon for the table.

During spring months the water is generally cold, but salmon will be found frequenting the upper ten to twenty feet. These fish are usually close to shore and within a mile or two of any river or creek mouth emptying into the Great Lakes or Pacific Ocean.

Little or no weight is needed to fish salmon at these depths. The lines are usually trolled flat (without downriggers) and about eighty to a hundred feet off the stern. A more rapid trolling speed can be used than during summer or fall months since the fish are actively feeding and will often chase a lure some distance before striking.

Small drab or dull-finished lures will produce the bulk of the strikes. I give the nod to Dardevle Imps, Thindevles, Cop-E-Cat Jr., Cop-E-Cat Imp, Devle Dog and Devle Dog Jrs. in brass with yellow and red diamonds, brass and orange potato bug, chartreuse with red spots and nickel inside, nickel and mackerel finish, nickel inside and shad (alewife) scale outside, and nickel inside and half-nickel–half-blue.

Attractors usually aren't used during the springtime, although some fishermen have had success trolling the 1/0 Sagamore Flasher, minus the hooks, and a blue or green Koho fly on a ten- or twelve-inch leader.

One of the hottest locations for early spring salmon fishing is around warm water discharges from power plants. The warm water attracts bait fish, which in turn draw in schools of salmon. I've had excellent fishing off discharges like this as soon as the ice went out.

One of the hottest places to locate spring salmon is where a river or stream empties into the Great Lakes or Pacific. Usually a distinct color line will exist where the dirtier river water mixes with the clean lake or ocean water. I like to troll along the edge of the color line; salmon frequent these areas early in the spring.

Light line is the rule for spring fishing. Most anglers seldom use over eight-pound mono. Spring fishing also calls for a willingness to change lure colors or size; if one combination isn't producing, stay alert and switch to something else.

Some of the most promising fishing, in the Great Lakes states at least, is pier fishing for spring salmon. The fish's proclivity for moving in close to shore after ice-out puts them within casting distance of pier fishermen. Light spinning tackle is used, and nickel or half-nickel–half-blue Devle Dogs are popular lures. The action can be fast-paced when a school of coho or chinook move in. A standard retrieve works best.

During summer months salmon are usually found in much deeper water. They show a decided preference for schooling over depths of at least 100 feet. A sensitive water temperature gauge should be used several times daily to pinpoint the exact depth of the fifty-four degree water preferred by these fish.

Deepwater fishing usually means downrigger fishing, at least in the Great Lakes. Downriggers allow the fisherman to set his lines at any

*Downriggers are often the key to getting one's Dardevles down to the proper level and keeping them there.*

depth, and a release system allows the fish to strike the lure and pull the line away from the cannonball so that the fisherman can play his salmon on a weight-free line.

It is vitally important for a midsummer salmon fisherman to use some type of sonar unit. Many anglers have gone to the more expensive straight line recording graphs which mark schools of fish on sensitive paper. With a rig like this spotting fish for you, it becomes easy to lower the proper Dardevle to the strike zone.

When salmon are found in depths of 60 to 120 feet, it takes a proper combination of lures and colors to turn them on. These fish show a decided preference for bright, hot colors such as green, blue, nickel, chartreuse with red spots, and pink.

For early summer (July and August) I suggest a smaller lure with plenty of fish-appealing action. Thindevles, Jr. Flutter Devles or the 1/0 Sagamore are my choices. These lures produce exciting action when trolled three to six feet behind a downrigger's cannonball. I've taken many limit catches on them.

Summer is an excellent time to fish with attractors and flies. I really like the Sagamore Flash and Koho fly during this period.

Green, dark blue, light pink and black flies have been my most productive colors. No one has been able to successfully explain the reason why salmon go for black lures or flies; but once in a while, when the fish have been pounded hard by fishermen and won't strike other colors, a switch to a black fly seems to turn the trick.

Most of the time a Sagamore Flash and Koho fly should be trolled about three feet behind the downrigger's cannonball. Occasionally, when the salmon schools are being pressured hard, the fish become more wary and you may have to fish further back from the cannonball.

I've seen times when it has become necessary to fish fifty or sixty feet behind the boat with downriggers. The basic reason for using an attractor such as Sagamore Flash is to entice the salmon to follow the fly. But the attractor must be rolling sideways, back and forth, to be effective; and this means the attractor must have something solid to pull against to produce the rolling action. Once the attractor and fly are run fifty or sixty feet behind the boat, however, they no longer provide tempting action since there is nothing solid to pull again. To remedy this I add a two- or three-ounce keel sinker about two feet ahead of the attractor. This offers just enough weight to give the attractor something to work against.

Ed Eppinger and his crew at the Dardevle plant have spent countless hours devising winning salmon combinations on lures. Most of the time the Koho fly, with its sixteen-inch leader, is good enough. I've found, however, that shortening the leader to eight or ten inches makes the lure much more effective.

Downrigger fishing is much more than simply attaching the fishing line to a downrigger release and lowering it to the proper depth. Fishermen have long ago learned that it pays to stagger downrigger lines just above the salmon's level. The fish will come up to strike a lure but will seldom go down after it.

If the fish are schooled between fifty and sixty feet, for instance, we'll usually fish downrigger lines at forty-five, forty-eight, fifty and fifty-two feet. In this manner most of the lures will be placed either just above the salmon or right at their level.

Both coho and chinook salmon are great lure followers. I've been able to watch salmon on my recording graph as they followed a lure for 100 to 200 yards without striking. But the angler must know how to convert followers into striking fish.

If your graph shows salmon moving slowly behind a lure, rapidly crank the cannonball up and down three or four feet at a time. This will rapidly pull the lure away from the fish, making it appear to be trying to get away. This often triggers a reflexive strike from the fish.

Some downriggers have movable arms. If this is true of your rig, another trick you can use is to rapidly raise and lower the downrigger arm, which will activate the lure.

I've been able to turn following salmon into strikers by simply making a short, sharp turn to port or starboard. This will cause the lures on the outside of the turn to change direction quickly and will raise them slightly in the water.

Another trick that works is to give the boat's engines a sudden burst of speed for several feet, causing the lures to swim quickly upwards for a few feet and then flutter back down as the boat slows to a normal trolling speed.

Downrigger tricks are something every salmon fisherman should employ when fishing gets tough.

As mid-August arrives, more and more salmon will be headed for the rivers in anticipation of their fall spawning period. The fish will usually be stacked up like cordwood, and limit catches of silvery salmon can be a daily possibility. The fish are at the peak of their weight and have become tremendous fighters. It takes a hot-colored lure and/or attractor to turn one of these fish into a twisting aerial fighter.

I'll often switch to the Sagamore Flash with nickel inside and Glo'in; nickel and chartreuse with red spots; or nickel and fluorescent red or orange with black spots. Team that with a yellow, pink, green or orange Koho fly and you'll be in business.

Other lures that are productive are the Dardevlet, Rok't Devle Imp, Cop-E-Cat Jr., Devle Dog, 2/0 Sagamore, Seadevle Imp and the King Flutter Devle.

My color selections for late summer and early fall salmon fishing are red with white stripe, Glo'in, yellow with five red diamonds, orange potato bugs, pink, chartreuse with red spots, red with yellow stripe, and fluorescent orange or green.

Coho and chinook often lie along the deepwater side of an underwater bank or drop-off. A trolling tactic that works is to troll parallel to the drop-off, circle back, and then work the lures over the edge of the drop-off. The salmon will often smack a lure as it drops over the edge of the bank.

Another trick that pays off when salmon have been fished hard near the mouth of a spawning stream is to troll lures clean without an attractor. Many times the flash of countless attractors will spook the salmon schools. A single lure, fished off a downrigger without an attractor, can be dynamite.

When schools of salmon scatter and just won't bite, try trolling in an entirely different area. Look for fish that haven't been pounded hard by fishermen and chances are you'll get into good fishing.

As schools of coho and chinook work in close to shore the wading fisherman can get a crack at them. For this type of fishing I prefer an open-faced spinning outfit stocked with twelve- to fifteen-pound mono. Nickel and blue, nickel or chartreuse-with-red-spot Devle Dogs, Dardevle Imp, Rok't Devle Imp or Cop-E-Cat Imp can be deadly medicine.

Cast out over the drop-off or into the rolling, porpoising salmon, and reel just fast enough to bring out the action. I occasionally allow the lure to flutter downward for a foot or two and then resume my retrieve. This is a deadly technique for prespawning salmon.

There are days when spoons won't interest the salmon, so I'll resort to a 1/4- or 1/2-ounce Notangle Spinner in nickel, nickel and blue, or chartreuse with red spots. A steady retrieve, one in which the spinner blade just flops over, is usually best, although I often alternate between a steady retrieve and a jerk-flutter-down retrieve. Both work.

You'll run into days when the fish seem to hover just out of casting range. When this happens I crimp a number four split shot onto the wire line tie; the extra weight permits a longer cast and increases the sinking time of the spinner without affecting the fish-catching qualities of the lure.

During late August, September and October, large schools of chinook appear in river systems small inland lakes tributary to the Great Leakes, and just offshore in the Pacific Ocean and the Great Lakes. This is prime time to catch trophy chinooks.

Dawn and dusk are two of the best times of day to catch these large salmon. I feel that trolling is the best method for hooking chinooks. I often fish four lines (off downriggers), and several times I have had two or three chinook on at once.

My best lures for chinook have been the yellow-with-five-red-diamonds or chartreuse-with-red-spot Dardevle, Seadevlet, Huskie Jr.,

*Ray Gilbert of Ontario hefts a gleaming silvery chinook salmon caught on a King Flutter Devle at South Haven, Michigan.*

and Troll Devle. The King Flutter Devle and 3/0 Sagamore have also been extremely productive for me.

I'll generally stagger my downrigger lines and place a different lure or color combination on each line until I learn the preference of the fish on that given day. Slow trolling is a must, and I'll often throttle down and head into the waves to decrease my speed.

If you're fishing with a handheld rod it pays to give it an occasional jerk, especially if you're using one of the thin spoons. This causes the lure to twist and dart in an erratic manner and it often drives chinook mad.

Another technique that pays off for chinook is a variation of the West Coast method of "mooching." On the Pacific they use fresh bait, but I've found Thin Devle or King Flutter Devle to be just as effective.

Locate the depth the chinook are using and spool the lure down to the fish from a stationary boat. When the lure is at the proper depth, give the engine a ten-foot burst of speed and then cut the engine back to neutral. This will cause the lure to swim rapidly toward the surface and then flutter back down to the salmon's level. If fish are present, this little-known trick will make them strike.

Salmon are spread throughout the Great Lakes and the Pacific from California north to Alaska. Excellent fishing exists in Wisconsin's waters of Lake Michigan from Milwaukee north to the Door Peninsula. The area around Sturgeon Bay is excellent for chinook.

Illinois produces some good fishing off Illinois Beach State Park and Diversey Harbor at Chicago.

Indiana's salmon fishing is confined primarily to the Michigan City area, but it's very good during the spring months.

Michigan has excellent salmon fishing along the entire Lake Michigan shoreline from Indiana north to the Upper Peninsula. Some of the best ports are South Haven, Saugatuck, Whitehall, Muskegon, Ludington, Manistee, Onekama, Arcadia, Frankfort, and Traverse City.

Good salmon fishing exists along Michigan's Lake Huron shoreline at Tawas City, Alabaster, Oscoda, Harrisville, Alpena, Rogers City, and Cheboygan.

Ohio has some fair salmon fishing in Lake Erie, as does the province of Ontario, especially during the fall months.

New York has good salmon fishing in Lake Erie near Dunkirk and Lake Ontario near Olcott, Wolcott, Oswego and Pulaski.

The area around Erie, Pennsylvania, provides fair to good salmon fishing in the waters of Lake Erie.

New Hampshire has been experimenting with coho plants in their limited portion of the Atlantic Ocean shoreline. Some good catches have been made near the seafront towns of Portsmouth and Hampton Beach. This area is largely overlooked.

Some salmon fishing is done in California around the towns of Eureka and Crescent City.

Good catches of salmon are made in Oregon near Gold Beach, Coos Bay, Newport, Pacific City, Barview, and Astoria.

*Author David Richey poses with a fifteen-pound Lake Michigan coho salmon taken on a Sagamore Flash and Koho fly.*

Washington has excellent salmon fishing at Ilwaco, Westport, Pacific Beach, Port Angeles and throughout the Strait of Juan De Fuca.

Some fantastic salmon fishing can be found in scattered locations around British Columbia's mainland and Vancouver Island. Some of the best producers are Knight Inlet and River's Inlet. Other hotspots are too numerous to mention.

Some excellent Alaskan salmon fishing exists from Petersburg north to

*Big chinook salmon like this dandy are the goal of many Pacific Ocean or Great Lakes fishermen.*

Anchorage. This is wild, unsettled country and few fishermen go out specifically for salmon. There are plenty of fish available in this region, but travel is mostly by plane or boat, and the costs are prohibitive for many fishermen.

## *Types of Retrieves*

Teaching a fisherman a new retrieve is like teaching an old dog new tricks. It can be done but only if the angler, or dog, is interested in learning.

The Dardevle brand of lures has an excellent fish-catching reputation in North America and around the world. Unfortunately, too many fishermen have adopted the "heave-'em-out-and-bring-'em-back" method of retrieve. This type of thinking results in far fewer fish taken than the fisherman would get if he tried experimenting with lure retrieval speeds.

Dardevles were designed to be used for all species of fish, both fresh and saltwater. They come in a variety of sizes, shapes and colors, and for every kind of fish there's a Dardevle with the appropriate action.

The most normal retrieve is to cast out a Dardevle, allow it to sink a few feet, and then reel it in at a moderate speed. Many fishermen never try any variations of this basic retrieve and thereby miss out on the fun of experimentation and an increased catch.

Another type of retrieve is one I've found useful many times for northern pike, especially in the spring, when the fish are in shallow water and foraging heavily on minnows. I call it the fast retrieve. Cast the spoon out and begin the retrieve before the lure hits the water. A high-speed retrieve ratio on a spinning reel is ideal for this type of fishing. Crank the reel handle as fast as possible and don't worry about a fish not being able to catch it; they can swim much faster than you can reel a Dardevle through the water.

I add another variation to this high-speed retrieve; I'll often impart an upward flipping motion to my rod tip which causes the lure to dart, wobble and jerk as it skips along just under the surface. I've often had strikes from early season bass and pike when the lure skittered right on

*This fisherman nets a scrappy brook trout from an unnamed lake in Quebec's bush country. It struck a Dardevle near the boat.*

top of the surface. The surface strikes this retrieve generates are visible and wrist-wrenching.

A slow retrieve should be included in any Dardevle fisherman's repertoire. This widely used method produces well for lake fish such as trout, bass, walleye, northern pike, muskellunge and, with smaller lures, panfish. Cast out, allow the lure to settle to the desired depth, and reel just fast enough to bring out the built-in wobble.

One spring I was fishing for steelhead in a northern Michigan lake and found the fish were attracted to a slow, deliberate retrieve. I caught more than thirty steelhead in one day with a slow retrieve and kept only two. Many times I could spot steelhead following the lure and see them strike almost at my feet.

I add another variation to the slow retrieve by giving it a bit of a jerk periodically. The lure will wobble in slowly, then dart upward or to one side as I jerk, and then resume the methodical wobble. Most strikes occur after the jerk when steady retrieving resumes.

Still another method of retrieving Dardevles is the darting motion. Cast out and let the lure settle to within a foot or two of bottom. Raise the rod tip to a vertical position with a sharp lift, reel up the slack line, and lower the rod tip to a horizontal position. Repeat the darting movement with the rod tip. I've used this technique many times for wise old bass and walleyes in heavily fished waters.

The deepwater retrieve is one of the most useful of all; it requires that the angler forget about losing Dardevles. He knows, when he begins his deepwater retrieve, that the method catches fish and often the largest fish. He also knows that bottom structure is going to exact a toll on his lure supply. If you're afraid of losing lures—and don't want to catch bragging-size fish—then forget this method.

The fisherman using the deepwater retrieve casts out and lets his spoon sink to bottom—I mean *right down on bottom.* Begin the retrieve by reeling very slowly and allow the lure to scratch its way back to you. The secret lies in working the lure slowly and right down among the rocks and other bottom debris. This works very well for covering the edges of steep drop-offs for walleyes or lake trout.

One time I had my children on a fishing trip to Everson's Lodge on Kabinakagami Lake north of Wawa, Ontario. The lake is a gold mine for delicious walleyes and I wanted my kids to get in on some hot fishing action. We scheduled a trip for midsummer, when walleye fishing is often best.

We encountered a lake with huge bays full of weeds. Such likely looking haunts for walleyes as drop-offs, gravel bars, points, and so on just didn't produce. After a full day of exploring I concluded that the walleyes had to be found near the weeds.

I tied a brass Dardevle Spinnie on each kid's line and we began a methodical search of the weed beds. We soon found small avenues of open water snaking through the weeds, and I was sure we'd at last discovered the haunt of some of the nice walleyes.

We anchored in the weeds parallel to one of these ten-foot-wide

*Pat Madigan unhooks a six-pound brook trout that hit a copper Devle Dog.*

stretches of open water. I instructed the kids to cast to the open water and allow the lures to sink all the way to bottom.

I next warned them to reel very slowly and just inch the spoons back to the boat. David, my oldest son, scored on his first cast with a sixteen-inch walleye that eased out of the weed beds and slapped hell out of his spoon.

We spent the rest of the day, and next four days, searching out weed beds with open water nearby. Each day we caught and released almost a hundred walleyes among us; none was over twenty inches in length, but the average was between sixteen and eighteen inches of the sweetest eating fish in the world. Again, it was a slow, deepwater retrieve that worked.

These are the basic types of retrieves used by most fishermen, but there are others that work under certain conditions. It's wise to know how and where to experiment with various retrieves.

Down Florida way jumbo large-mouth bass work into the shallows during March and April to spawn. They'll dig out redds under hyacinths, and the males are very protective of their beds. This is shallow-water fishing; you need chest-high waders, a sturdy spinning or baitcasting outfit, and rugged monofilament capable of turning ten-pound or better bass away from the lettuce.

My favorite lure for this type of fishing is either a feathered weedless Dardevle, feathered weedless Dardevlet, or a feathered weedless Dardevle Imp in nickel inside with black-and-white chunk. I've also had excellent success with copper-colored weedless Dardevles.

The technique is to wade along slowly and cast far ahead to the emergent clumps of weeds, reeds or hyacinths. Bass often bed directly beneath or alongside the vegetation. As soon as the weedless spoon hits the water, begin reeling with a frequent up-and-down motion of the rod tip. The lure will skitter along the top of the water, and bass literally climb all over the spoon. The retrieve has to be kept fast to keep it on top of the water.

Another variation with weedless Dardevles is to cast near the vegetation as you wade. Allow the lure to sink near bottom and ease it through the tangles of aquatic vegetation. Bass will strike as the lure swims through their beds.

In southern and southwestern bass lakes in Florida, Georgia, Oklahoma, Texas and Louisiana, a technique known locally as "doodlesocking" has proven highly successful. This is nothing more than a vertical jigging technique used when fishing in man-made reservoirs among the drowned trees and stickups. For jigging I like the Cop-E-Cat Jr., Cop-E-Cat Imp, or Seadevle Imp. These lures work well when lowered into the timber and jigged up and down in six- to twelve-inch pulls, or merely jigged upwards and allowed to flutter back down. It's important to keep the lure moving at all times and to jig straight up and down. Any sideways movement of the lure will often result in a tangle with the brush. I'll often substitute a hefty 1/0 or 2/0 single hook for the treble when doodlesocking in heavy brush.

The last time I tried this trick was on Sam Rayburn Reservoir in eastern Texas. We located a pile of drowned timber in fifteen feet of water, off an old creek channel. The sun was slanting off to the west, so we fished the west side of the timber, away from the sun.

We prospected in various places but finally settled on an area where the channel lay closest to the stickups. We lowered our Seadevle Imps into the tangle from an anchored boat and began a methodical jigging stroke.

My buddy made three or four vertical lifts on his rod tip, and suddenly the rod tip shot toward the water. He leaned heavily on the rod, pressed his thumb firmly against the reel's spool, and literally manhandled the bass out of the brush. The battle was short-lived because he wore that fish out in short order. Five minutes later he lipped a nine-pound bass into the boat, and twenty minutes after that I locked horns with a similar-sized bass. We stuck with that "honey hole" for two hours and kept a handpicked quartet of six- to nine-pound bass.

It's important for today's angler to realize that no one method of retrieve can cover all situations. Our angler must understand that he has to adapt and experiment with sinking times, methods of retrieval, and lure sizes, shapes and colors to be successful.

Without experimentation, no one can be consistently successful at fishing, even with Dardevles.

# *Tricks That Take Stubborn Fish*

Over the years, in my countless miles of travel to acquire material for magazine articles and books, I've run into several tricks that work when fish develop a bad case of lockjaw. These tricks work sometimes, none of the time, or always—depending on the fish, its habitat and its feeding habits.

One time I was fishing Kasagami Lake in northern Ontario, about forty-five miles southeast of James Bay, for giant northern pike. We'd had mediocre success with pike in the twelve- to fifteen-pound class but couldn't seem to locate anything larger.

Once we had a twenty-pound lunker leave the edge of a weed bed and chase the red and white Dardevle. The fish called off the attack and returned to his lair. We pegged cast after cast at the fish but he completely ignored our offerings.

I told my guide, "I think the fish went to sleep." His reply was a classic, and one I'd never heard before. "I'll wake him up and then he'll hit."

We upped the anchor and roared into the weed bed full bore. Then the Cree guide lifted the prop half our of the water and churned hell out of that shallow bay with the engine winding out at maximum RPMs. He bounced the boat and motor over, through, and around the weed bed while water flew in all directions. Apparently satisfied after five minutes of this water-churning commotion, he headed back out into open water, just a short cast away, and re-anchored. "He's awake now. Start casting!"

We snapped on bright new Dardevles and pegged casts into the shallows, although we were a bit skeptical about what we should expect. I thought the pike would be about five miles down the lake by now and still swimming hard to get away from the fury of the half-submerged outboard prop.

I halfheartedly began my retrieve when I felt a gentle nudge at my spoon. I set the hook but nothing happened. I was sure I'd temporarily fouled the lure on a piece of floating debris.

Ray's second cast dropped neatly into the water where we'd first seen the big pike make his appearance. He hadn't made two turns of the reel handle when the lure stopped with a sudden jolt. He slammed the rod tip back out of pure reflex, and again nothing happened. He said the lure seemed to be hung on bottom.

I watched as slowly—as if in slow motion—the tip of the pike's tail eased from the water and then submerged. "Hit him again!" I hollered. Ray jabbed the hooks home two more times and that shallow bay exploded with the fury of a big northern that just realized he'd been had.

The fish headed for deep water with the line hissing behind him. When he passed the boat that fish looked as long as an oar. Ray kept the line tight and the fish sounded for bottom in a power dive that literally smoked the mono from his reel. The drag was buzzing like a rattler on a hot rock, and Ray had his hands full.

Our guide lifted the anchor and we tussled with the fish for over fifteen minutes before the long snaky head broke the surface film, rolled its green body into a coil, and uncorked one of the finest aerial leaps I've had the pleasure of watching. Two minutes later the fish was done, completely tired out, and was led to the boat and landed.

Six hours later in camp the lanky pike scaled twenty pounds and was forty-four inches in length—a fine testimonial to "stirring up" reluctant fish. Since that time I've used the trick on northern pike on Lake Mistassini in Quebec, where it paid off with a twenty-four-pound pike on a nickel Dardevlet.

One time I was fishing for black crappie on Santee-Cooper Reservoir in South Carolina. The weather was hot and the crappies weren't biting well. We tried finding suspended fish, and worked the brush piles and other haunts; but our success amounted to a couple of under-sized specks which weren't large enough to smell up a frying pan, let alone make a respectable stringer of fish for photos.

I decided to try an old Michigan perch fishing trick of offering the fish a pair of lures instead of only one. I had a "perch spreader," a wire frame capable of holding two lines instead of one, and I attached one Lil' Devle to each line. One was hammered nickel and the other was a nickel inside and blue herring scale on the outside.

We anchored over what was known locally as a "crappie hole." I attached a 1/8-ounce bell sinker to the bottom end of the spreader and

*This fisherman gills an eighteen-pound northern pike which struck a Dardevle fished on High Rock Lake, Manitoba.*

lowered it to bottom. Once the line was tight and straight beneath the boat I began jigging the spreader and two lures straight up and down in smooth, six-inch pulls. After about five minutes of continuous jigging I felt the technique wasn't going to work and was about ready to suggest a change of scenery when my rod tip bent over under the force of a hefty strike.

I began bringing the fish to the surface, but the fight felt strange. It felt as if I had the grandaddy of all crappies on and the fight seemed to be going in two directions at once.

I remembered the crappie's delicate mouth and played the fish with caution, giving line whenever I had to. Shortly the fish could be seen circling beneath the boat, and as I brought it to the boat I saw a second hooked fish on the bottom lure.

In short order we'd changed our day from dull inactivity to one with plenty of action. We went on to catch another dozen crappies in the 1½- to-2½-pound class within the hour.

The perch spreader technique will work on crappies and perch, and occasionally on bluegills and other schooling fish. The important thing is to present Dardevle lures in a size usually productive for the game fish you're trying to catch. It doesn't accomplish much to offer a much-too-large lure for smaller game fish.

Much has been mentioned about a muskie's willingness to follow a lure right up to the boat and then call off the pursuit. But few fishermen realize that big trout and northern pike also follow lures for some distance without striking.

Another time I was fishing in a small private lake in Quebec for brook trout. The brookies would work up from the depths and follow the lure into shallow water but seldom strike. They were interested, but something was wrong.

I finally decided to try the old muskie trick of doing a figure eight with my Devle Dog near the boat. The jumbo brook trout was hanging back about ten feet from the boat and wouldn't come any closer.

As the lure neared the boat, I slowed down the retrieve and began doing a circular figure eight. The fish seemed interested. I was about ready to give this up as a bad guess when a brookie darted in and scooped the lure into his mouth with a flash of white-edged fins. I set the hook and the fight was on.

The battle was a humdinger, lasting nearly ten minutes, and complete with the bulldogging scrap big brookies are noted for. I finally led the fish to the net and hung him on a pair of hand-held scales. The needle quivered and finally settled on six pounds—a dandy trophy for an unusual trick.

I've since tried this method on other brook trout lakes with absolutely no success. So even though it doesn't always work, it's a useful tidbit of information to have when other techniques fail.

I've used this particular technique with much better success on large northern pike, particularly in remote Canadian lakes.

Once I was fishing Manitoba's High Rock Lake and the action was slow. We drifted into a shallow bay with a pair of chunky walleyes hanging over the edge. We were looking ahead for signs of cruising northerns when a sudden splash next to the boat caused us to look down. A big northern had one of our walleyes in his mouth and was shaking it like a terrier with a rat.

Cory Kilvert, a fishing buddy of mine, dropped a short cast over the side of the boat and began doing a figure eight with his Dardevle. The

*Cory Kilvert poses with a beautiful northern pike on Manitoba's High Rock Lake.*

pike dropped the walleye, closed to within six inches of the wobbling spoon, and eyed it with an angry glare. Cory kept up his figure-eight routine; and the pike eased up to the lure, took it sideways in its mouth, and held on as Cory pounded the hooks home. The fish began shaking and twisting, apparently thinking this was some new type of walleye that was fighting back.

The pike finally decided something was wrong and arrowed for deep water. Cory fought the fish like a pro, and finally we were able to lead the fish to the net, where we landed a twenty-two pound northern. A genuine trophy for a unique method of pike fishing. Fishing is never the constant action one finds in spectator sports. Many variables enter into the picture, and the fisherman must be versatile and willing to constantly experiment with various tricks. It's true that these tricks for stubborn fish may not work for you. But again they may work, and if they add just one more fish to your catch over a lifetime, they were worth reading and well worth trying.

# *Northern Pike and Muskies*

The northern pike and muskellunge of North America represent two of the most prized trophies commonly sought by anglers. These fish grow to large sizes and provide a tremendous battle on spinning or baitcasting tackle. Fishermen are constantly on the lookout for new hot spots.

Both fish are predatory in nature, and anything that swims, flies or lands in the water nearby can become a quick meal for a ravenous fish.

Although the northern and the muskellunge are similar in appearance and often confused by inexperienced anglers, they have many distinguishing features. Pike are very elongated, with large, flat heads and tooth-studded jaws, but have scales only on the upper half of the gill cover and the entire cheek, while the muskellunge has scales only on the top half of the cheek and gill cover. Northerns usually have five mandibular (lower jaw) sensory pores, while a muskellunge has six to nine. This can be a quick, easy identification between these look-alike species.

Coloration of northerns and muskellunge (the latter come in three subspecies) varies considerably from one area to another. The standard appearance of a pike is a dark green back which shades to a light green on the sides and a white belly. The sides are conspicuously spotted with bean-shaped yellowish spots, and the fins are heavily spotted.

There are other color patterns in northerns. I've seen many anadromous northern pike, ascending streams tributary to the Great Lakes, which are silvery from their existence in open water. Silver pike are found in certain areas of Minnesota, Manitoba, the Northwest Territories, Sweden and a couple of lakes in northeastern Ontario.

The three subspecies of muskellunge commonly sought by sportsmen are the northern (Wisconsin strain), Great Lakes, and tiger. The Great Lakes subspecies is indigenous to the Great Lakes watershed and occurs in certain inland lakes in Michigan and in Lake St. Clair, the boundary

*These fishermen admire a near-twenty-pound northern pike taken from Savant Lake, Ontario, by casting Dardevles.*

between Michigan and Ontario. Great Lakes muskies are heavily spotted.

The northern muskie is a fish common to northern Michigan, Wisconsin, Minnesota, and some Ontario lakes. Its sides are of a dull color.

The tiger muskie is a cross between the northern Wisconsin muskie and a northern pike; it has faint stripes running parallel to the lateral line.

Both pike and muskies spawn during the spring, but pike usually spawn much earlier in the season. Depending on the climate, northerns will usually spawn between March and early May, while muskellunge normally go about their spawning chores anytime from April through early June.

*A sixteen-pound northern comes to the net for Ray Gilbert on Ontario's Savant Lake.*

The habitat normally preferred by northern pike would be along any dense weed bed, along a sharp drop-off into deep water, or near a submerged brush pile or downed tree lying close to shore. The muskie, however, will often take up residence in deeper water off a submerged reef or sunken island, in a heavy patch of muskie or pickerel weeds, near the mouth of a river, or in a deep channel running through a lake.

Both species are opportunistic feeders and will chow down on almost anything they can get into their mouths including a variety of smaller fish, snakes, small ducks, frogs, and salamanders.

Most northern pike caught in North America will be taken from water

*Stan Bowles lands a busted-net northern pike for Cory Kilvert on Manitoba's High Rock Lake.*

less than fifteen feet deep, while evidence shows the muskellunge will often inhabit depths of up to forty or fifty feet during hot summer months.

Tricks that will consistently take northern pike often fail to interest a muskie. One year I was fishing High Rock Lake in northern Manitoba, and the pike were in the shallows chasing spawning suckers. The water is only three or four feet deep, and the fish were systematically conducting a slaughter. A normal retrieve where the red and white Dardevle would sink a foot or two and wobble back simply didn't interest the fish.

I tried for an hour to coax the fish into striking, but it was no use. Small fish were skittering to the surface as the northerns bulged the water below them in a feeding frenzy.

I finally tried beginning my retrieve before the spoon hit the water. I cranked the handle of my spinning reel furiously, and the lure skittered across the surface like the hapless bait fish. The water parted, a toothy maw rolled behind the spoon, and it disappeared in a shower of spray. I set the hooks and held on as a large pike thundered off for deep water.

Fifteen minutes later we slid the meshes around a twenty-one-pound northern. Within three hours, two of us landed our limits of trophy northerns weighing from fifteen to twenty-nine pounds. Every fish struck the fast, skittering retrieve across the surface.

Simply trolling back and forth through proven habitat takes many

*Dardevles are winners for twenty-pound pike like this one posed by Cory Kilvert.*

*A leaping northern pike drenches this angler with spray.*

*Stan Bowles (left) and Cory Kilvert pose with three trophy-size northern pike from High Rock Lake.*

pike throughout their range. I normally select either a standard Dardevle, Dardevlet, Seadevlet, Cop-E-Cat Jr., or Troll Devle. Although the red and white stripe with a nickel back has universally been the most popular pike color, I've had tremendous success with the same color with a brass back. The yellow with five red diamonds has consistently proven itself for me as has the chartreuse with red spots and a nickel inside.

Other popular lure colors have been the crackle frog with a nickel inside, black and white stripe with nickel back, and the orange and green perch scale with either nickel or brass inside.

I'd much rather cast spoons than troll, and casting often allows the fisherman a chance to work areas a boat can't get into. Many times I'll motor upwind of a productive-looking area, then drift down the lake and cast to likely areas.

I enjoy whipping Dardevles back into open pockets in the reeds. One time I was wind-drifting Chequamegon Bay in northern Wisconsin and methodically casting into the reeds. An hour had passed and I hadn't seen a northern or had a strike. I passed by a larger-than-normal pocket and probed it with two casts. The second cast lit with a dainty splash, and a big pike caught it like an outfielder going after a fly ball. My rod tip smashed down with the force of the strike, and I held on as the fish rampaged back and forth through the shallows. Several minutes later I managed to work the fish out into open water and finally brought him close enough to lift into the boat. He was the first of three trophy northerns I caught that day that ranged from fourteen to seventeen and one half pounds. Every hit occurred when I'd cast into the reeds and retrieve quickly to simulate a bait fish fleeing for its life.

Another method of wind-drifting that pays off is to peg casts alongside submerged treetops or logs lying along the shoreline. This technique once paid off with several pike in the twelve-to-nineteen-pound class from Ontario's Batchewana River. The fish would nose out from under the logs or brush, follow the Dardevle for several feet, and the launch a savage attack on the spoon.

Another Dardevle trick I use is to cast the spoon near a submerged weed bed, allow it to sink on a tight line, and then give it a helluva jerk to start it moving. I reel up the slack line, allow it to settle for a five count, and give another healthy upward jerk on the rod tip. This really turns on big pike.

Once in a while, when pike seem turned off by any type of retrieve, I'll attach a four-inch strip of pork rind to a Dardevle. I cast this out and reel it in very slowly, just fast enough to bring out the wobble. The pork rind slithers along behind and actually teases fish into striking.

A method of fishing Dardevles that works at times is to cast out, allow the lure to settle briefly, and then work it back to the boat with a series of jerks and quick retrieves. The lure should never stop moving.

*Twilight over northern pike country.*

Northern pike range from New York westward through the Great Lakes states, into Missouri, Nebraska, and parts of Iowa; and they have been transplanted into western states such as Montana, Arizona and Colorado.

In Canada northern pike are distributed from Labrador westward through Quebec, Ontario, the prairie provinces of Alberta, Saskatchewan and Manitoba, northward into the Yukon and the Northwest Territories, and then westward into Alaska.

Alaska offers excellent pike in many waters, although the fish, as a rule, are on the small side. Try fishing the area between the Alaska and Brooks ranges.

Colorado has some excellent pike in Bonny Reservoir, Boyd Reservoir and Queens Reservoir.

Good fishing occurs in Iowa's Lake Okoboji, Storm Lake and in many of the wing dam areas along the Mississippi River. Michigan offers a raft of good fishing on scattered Great Lakes bays such as Keweenaw, Huron, Tawas, Thunder and Saginaw and on inland lakes such as Bond Falls Flowage, AuTrain Basin, Houghton Lake, Big and Little Bay De Noc, Bad River, and Manistee Lake. Wisconsin has good pike fishing in Big Round, Lac Vieux Desert, Pelican, Lake Winnebago, Lake Paygan, the Mississippi and Wolf rivers, and in Chequamegon Bay.

Big pike producers in Minnesota are Lake of the Woods, Red Lake, Lake Winnibigoshish, Mille Lacs and Leech Lake as well as many others.

My favorite Canadian pike producers are Ontario's Lake of the Woods, Little Vermilion, Savant, Kasagami, Eagle and Rainy. Quebec has an untapped pike fishery in Mistassini and Laverendrye Parks as well as near Club Chambeaux in the Kaniapiscau River. Saskatchewan offers Lake Athabasca, Lac La Ronge, Reindeer and Black. Manitoba has excellent fishing in High Rock Lake, Gods Lake, Lake Athapapuskow, Gods River and Island Lake.

Alberta has big pike in Great Slave, Lake Athabasca, Hay, Wabasca, Loon, and Namur Lakes. Fishermen traveling to the Northwest Territories often overlook excellent pike fishing in Great Bear Lake (I once caught a huge eighteen-pound northern from Bransons Lodge while lake trout fishing), Great Slave Lake and the McKenzie River system. Many lakes have an unknown pike fishery available for sportsmen to explore.

The Yukon offers good pike fishing in many lakes and rivers, although most anglers are intent on other species. I'd suggest Nisutlin River or Teslin Lake.

Pike and muskie fishing demand good line. Many experts swear by a twelve-inch wire leader testing about twenty pounds. I prefer using a twenty-pound mono for most of my pike and muskie fishing, especially for trophies, and I've never had a pike or muskie cut my line with its teeth.

If you prefer using lighter mono then add a shock tippet of twenty-pound mono or a wire leader; it can spell the difference between landing your trophy and losing it to a frayed line.

The muskie fisherman is one totally resolved to spending long hard hours on the lake casting for his fish. True, some fish are caught on live bait or by trolling, but they are dull, uninteresting methods of fishing.

Most muskie anglers are stand-up fisherman, clothed with long-brimmed baseball caps and polarized sunglasses to cut glare and enable them to spot following fish. Muskies often pursue a lure for long distances without striking, and the observant angler that can spot a trailing muskie is often the best fisherman on the lake.

A following muskie often gives a fisherman his first clue to the whereabouts of fish in any given body of water. A muskie is curious and will often pace a lure right up to the boat with his savage, pointed snout six inches behind a spoon or spinner.

Old-timers say the best response whenever a muskie peels out of a weed bed and trails closely behind a lure is to hasten the retrieve. This worked one time for me on Wisconsin's Tomahawk Lake. I spotted the fish and rapidly began cranking harder on my reel. The Huskie Jr. sped forward and the muskie had the lure instantly. He swirled sideways as he grabbed the spoon, splashed the surface with his tail, and headed back for the weeds. I slammed the hooks home three times and watched, in awe, as the twenty-two-pound fish vaulted into the air, threw his head sideways half a dozen times, and then smashed back into the lake. Six jumps later he was led to the waiting net.

Another trick for following muskies is to do a figure eight with the lure right next to the boat. I've tried this tactic countless times without success, although many guides believe in it.

I've found, over the years, that following muskies seldom strike. The strikes you get often come from beneath the lure as the fish arrows up off bottom and hammers the lure.

One of the most successful muskie methods is called "fast trolling." I select a Huskie Devle or a Troll Devle and attach a two-ounce keel sinker about two feet ahead of the lure. Troll at a moderately fast speed parallel to the outside edges of weed beds or crisscross back and forth off the deepwater edges of the weeds. Muskies are suckers for a lure speeding past their lair, and this method has really caught on in many portions of their range.

The best colors for speed trolling lures are red-white stripe with nickel inside, black-white stripe with nickel back, orange-green perch scale with nickel or brass inside, and black-yellow stripe with a nickel or brass back.

*A big Dardevle suckered this muskie into striking.*

Spinner baits have long been a favorite of muskie fishermen. These lures have a large following for one reason; they produce fish on a consistent basis.

The Notangle Spinner in the half-ounce size and the world famous J.T. Buel Fluted Spinner in sizes 1/0, 2/0 and 3/0 are my favorites for casting to cagy muskies. The feathered or bucktail spinners are most popular since muskies show a decided preference for spinners with a dressed treble hook. The colors that have produced best for me have been black and white stripe with nickel inside; red and white stripe with nickel inside; orange and black spotted chunk with nickel back; and a hand-painted all black spinner blade.

One of the fascinating aspects of fishing the Notangle, and Fluted Spinner is the unique bend which prevents line twist. I'm sure Ed Eppinger didn't plan his bend to be used for the following trick, but it's one I've used successfully many times. If extra depth is needed to get down to a muskie hideout, attach either one or two split shot to the bend in the wire or firmly crimp on a RubberCor sinker weighing about a half ounce. This extra weight allows for extra casting distance and greatly hastens the sinking time. The sinker or split shot doesn't affect the action of the spinner.

*Once hooked, muskies are aerial battlers and this Ontario muskie is giving the angler fits.*

I usually anchor along the outside edge of a heavy weed patch, after a quiet approach, and cast the spinner parallel to the outside edges of the weeds or into the edges of the salad and slowly work the spinner back to the boat. Once the spinner passes the outside edge of the weed bed, allow it to sink on a tight line for several feet and begin a retrieve that brings out the throbbing beat of the spinner blade. Occasionally I'll alternate by giving the spinner a hefty reef with my rod tip, allowing it to sink while I reel in excess line, and then reefing again.

Another spinner technique that works at times is to cast right smack into the middle of a weed bed. Keep the rod tip high, reel fast, and literally rip the spinner through the weeds. I've seen muskies tear a weed bed apart to home in on the struggling spinner. More than once I've seen a muskie smack the lure with a foot or more of weeds trailing behind.

Another deadly method has been devised for following muskies. Practitioners in Wisconsin call it the crisscross method. Two anglers stand in an anchored or drifting boat and deliberately cast across each other's line. The lures, usually a Huskie Devle and a large Fluted Spinner, are retrieved so that one crosses directly in front of the other. A trailing muskie, intent on following one lure, suddenly sees another lure, which it may assume is another predatory fish, and strikes one or the other out of anger, territorial instinct, or sheer meanness. The method demands the utmost in angler concentration and two fishermen highly skilled in the technique; but it often works when other methods fail to produce fish.

All three subspecies of muskie are found throughout the northern tier of states east of the Mississippi River, with the greatest abundance of fish being found in Michigan, Wisconsin, Minnesota and Ontario. Scattered good fishing occurs in New York, Pennsylvania, Tennessee, West Virginia, Kentucky and Ohio.

Hot spots which have produced for me and for several of my friends are Lake St. Clair, Indian River, Brevort Lake, Thornapple Lake, St. Clair River, Iron Lake and Elk Lake in Michigan; Chippewa Flowage, Tomahawk Lake, Lac Court Oreilles, Flambeau Flowage and Lake Pokegama in Wisconsin; Leech Lake and Lake Winnibigoshish in Minnesota; and in Ontario such excellent muskie waters as Lake of the Woods, Eagle Lake, Lake St. Clair, St. Clair River and parts of the St. Lawrence River.

Other lesser-known but productive locations are the St. Lawrence River, Chautauqua Lake and Black Lake in New York; the Muskingum River and Ricky Fork Lake in Ohio; Daddys Creek, Crab Orchard Lake and Dale Hollow Lake in Tennessee; the Ohio River, Green River and Barren River in Kentucky; West Virginia's Middle Island Creek and the Pocatiligo River; and Pennsylvania's Presque Isle Bay in Lake Erie, Conneaut Lake, Pymatuning Dam and the Shenango River.

# *A New Look at the Dardevle Klicker*

Back in the 1930s a fishing lure swept the nation because of its innovative new twist: a set of whirling willow leaves attached to the back of a spoon. The spoon enjoyed popularity for a generation and then gradually faded into oblivion. Now the Eppinger Manufacturing Company has reissued the Dardevle Klicker, the Dardevlet Klicker and the Dardevle Imp Klicker. These lures have been taking game fish consistently since their reintroduction.

Many fishermen already know just how deadly Dardevle lures can be, but few have learned just how devastating the effect of a flashing Klicker can be on most species of fish.

Most game-fish species feed either by sight, sound, smell or taste; but biologists and research fishermen have discovered that most freshwater fish rely mostly on sight and sound when foraging on smaller bait fish.

The flashing sides of a bait fish have been known to draw game fish from some distance, and many fish home in to a free meal because the stimulus received by their eyes is relayed directly to their brain as FOOD. It has been proven conclusively that the flashing wobble of a Dardevle has a built-in attraction to most fish species and this flash, wobble or throb of a darting lure simulates something game fish are used to feeding on. Once you combine the normal action of a Dardevle with the flutter and sound of the whirling willow leaf blades, you've got a double-barrel attraction few fish can ignore.

The second method by which many game fish home in on a struggling baitfish is by means of sound—vibrations transmitted through the water. Predatory fish such as trout, salmon, pike, muskellunge, bluefish, striped bass, largemouth or smallmouth bass, walleyes and sauger all feed heavily on baitfish; and they are accustomed to seeing and hearing the vibration and wobble of a disabled forage fish.

*The Dardevle Klicker and these two fishermen teamed up to boat this big northern pike.*

The three types of Dardevle Klickers simply add another inducement for gamefish to strike. Whereas most lures rely solely on the visible action of the lure, the Klickers give off both sound and flash, greatly increasing the number of strikes.

A year ago I was fishing Quebec's Lake Mistassini for the huge northern pike I'd heard frequented the area. I had a dozen Dardevle Klickers along with red and white stripe backs and nickel inside. I long ago learned this seems to be the best color combination for pike.

We were easing down a spruce-studded shoreline and casting Dardevle Klickers randomly along the edges of trees toppled into the lake. My wife, Kay, said, "I just saw a fish boil beneath that leaning tree." To punctuate her remarks she rifled a cast alongside the drowned tree branches. The water boiled again and she felt a solid jolt as the fish ravaged the spoon.

She banged the hooks home and held onto her spinning rod as it buckled under the force of the fish's first run. "He's big!" she muttered between tightly clenched teeth (she gets determined when a fish is giving her a hard time). It tried once to jump, and she pulled it off balance, making it topple heavily back into the water.

The big northern tried to peel under the boat, but she expertly slid the line over the bow and continued battling the big fish on short line. I was trying for pictures, and the pike was jumping and splashing so close that it covered my camera lens with water.

After a short-lived but spirited struggle, Kay led the fish to the boat,

*Stan Bowles, owner-operator of Athapapuskow Lodge in Manitoba, is a firm believer in the Dardevle Klicker for taking big pike from his remote outpost camp on High Rock Lake.*

*The author poses with two pike in the eighteen-pound class which struck a Dardevlet Klicker in Quebec's Lake Mistassini.*

where I got a firm grip across its gills and lifted it in. We hung the big pike on hand-held scales just long enough to record its weight at 17½ pounds before releasing it back into the lake.

That trip was an eye-opener for Kay and me as to the unique fish-catching qualities of the Dardevle Klicker. We switched around among the three sizes of Klicker and found they all produced equally well.

Another time Kay and I were wading and casting the shoreline of a large brown trout lake. The fish had been in the shallows for a week and were expected soon to depart for deeper water with the advent of warmer weather.

We waded out about dark, and she went one way while I drifted the other. Darkness was complete and neither of us had a strike. We met about an hour later and compared notes. She asked, "What's wrong? The fish should be working the shallows right now!"

We'd been tossing assorted lures and hadn't had a follow. I suggested a dark lure; and she said, "How about a Dardevle Imp Klicker in black and white chunk? The browns will be able to see the dark color against the sky, and the Klicker will give off sound waves and flash in the water." It sounded like a beautiful idea.

We had two Imp Klickers in black and white chunk, so she took one and I knotted the other to my line. We separated again and I watched her wade down to a large point jutting into deep water and begin casting.

I'd just turned my back and begun fishing when I heard Kay yell. The moon was just peeking over wood-clad hills, and her rod was silhouetted against the dark shore as she stood firm and battled a heavy fish in the darkness.

I sidled down to her and listened as she talked to the fish. "C'mon, big fella. A little closer, just a little closer." The brown was boring for bottom, but she'd had the fish on for almost ten minutes, and it was growing tired of fighting the bend of her rod.

Tiny slivers of water sprayed upwards against the faint glow of the moon. The fish tried to surface and jump, but it was too tired. Kay finally backed towards shore and slid the trout over my landing net; and our first fish, a five-pounder, had met its fate by tangling with a Klicker lure.

Kay and I caught four other browns that evening before a fog rolled

*These fishermen made a fine catch of brown trout by wading a trout lake after dark and casting Dardevle Imp Klickers.*

over the lake and the fish went down. Our biggest was a 5½-pounder, but none was under three pounds. Every fish, feeding by sight and sound, had inhaled the lures deeply.

There are many situations where the Klicker lures would come in handy. I've seen these lures produce well at night and in turbid or muddy water where the sound waves are more important than sight. They've done well by me for both lake and river fishing.

The retrieve is always important, and Dardevle Klickers lend themselves well to any type of retrieve. One of the most productive, in my opinion, is the jerk-pause-retrieve method, in which the lure is cast out, allowed to sink briefly, and then started back. I'll usually give the rod tip a jerk to make the willow leaves flutter enticingly, pause the retrieve for about a second, during which the lure flutters down, and then begin the retrieve again. Reel up the slack line, jerk, pause, and retrieve. This technique has proven successful for a variety of game fish.

The standard slow retrieve that just brings out the wobble of the spoon is also a standby whenever I fish the lure. The wobble gives the spoon just enough motion to allow the willow leaves to flutter behind.

I've found that most game fish will engulf the lure, and this seems to be caused by the fish striking toward the spinners. They try to attack the whole lure, spinners and all. I've taken walleyes and northern pike with the entire lure buried in their gills.

The Dardevle Klicker family is a welcome asset to the fisherman's bag of tricks. This is one of the brightest lures a fisherman can try this year.

## How Dardevles Are Made

Craftsmanship is important when it comes to fishing lures. It shows up in such areas as correct action, life of the finish, ease of casting, and the success in fishing. For nearly seventy years Dardevles have been made by skilled workmen from the finest quality materials. The Eppinger folks are proud of their products and of the way they perform.

To begin a lure, premium grade copper and brass strips are "spanked" in an operation that forms the metal into varying thicknesses. Perfection is important, since subtle variations affect balance and weight, factors important in preventing line twisting or spinning.

Creating the final shape is equally demanding. Different plane surfaces and curves are required for different model Dardevles since these are responsible for each lure's unique action.

After the lure is shaped, ground and polished smooth, it is prepared for a final coating of tough-finish metal which is electroplated to the base. Most lures receive three platings. Final polishing gives a smoothly finished lure that often means the difference between a missed strike and a hooked fish.

Only one paint has been found to stand up to the rough workout fish (and fishermen) give Dardevles. This almost indestructible enamel goes on in five coats to provide a nearly chip-proof and fade-proof finish. Each coat is baked to give added protection and to assure the bright, durable colors that attract fish.

The same emphasis on quality that has marked each Dardevle from the beginning is used to select the hooks. The manufacturer looks for sharpness and strength enough for tough-jawed muskies and pike when they choose hooks for Dardevles.

Throughout a long history of lure making, Eppinger Manufacturing Company has strived to provide anglers with the best possible fishing lures. This dedication is unswerving, since helping you catch fish is their most important business.

# *Rainbow and Brown Trout Tactics*

Two of the trout species most popular among anglers are the rainbow and brown. Rainbows receive wide acclaim from fishermen for their willingness to take lures and for their aerial acrobatics, while the browns draw admirers because of their shy, retiring manner and hefty size.

Many fishermen think of Dardevles as pike lures; but there are various sizes and shapes of this brand of lure that are designed for trout fishing, whether in an inland lake or a stream.

One warm spring a few years ago I was wading along Bear Lake in northern Michigan casting for cruising rainbows. The fish were feeding heavily on minnows in the shallows, and it seemed duck soup to cast ahead of the wakes and expect a heavy strike.

I spooled up with six-pound mono, tied a silver Devle Dog Jr. onto the light line, and began wading and fan-casting ahead of me. Several fish spooked away from the dainty splash of the lure, and I wondered if the lure was too large.

An hour went by and I hadn't had a strike, although several fish swirled at the lure before backing away. It finally dawned on me that with the bright overhead sun the lure color must be wrong—probably too much flash in the shallow water. I knotted on a copper Devle Dog Jr. and immediately began obtaining strikes.

One fish grabbed the lure and raced off for deep water as my drag howled in pain. I kept the rod tip high and forced the fish to battle the tightly bowed rod. Five minutes later I led a chunky, five-pound rainbow to the beach and slipped him on my stringer. The fish had hit a jerk-pause retrieve in two feet of water.

Within a matter of three hours I'd landed my limit of five trout, and the smallest fish was a fat sixteen-incher that scaled three pounds. I'd hooked and lost two fish that would have been more than six pounds each.

*Jumping brown trout can be yours if you fish Devle Dogs when the fish work in close to the shallows.*

*Wading fisherman poses with a 15½-pound brown trout taken on a Devle Dog Jr.*

Lake fishing techniques work well for rainbow trout. The fish are normally much heavier than a typical stream rainbow and they are used to feeding voraciously on small bait fish. In the smaller sizes, any of the Dardevle lures is appropriate for this type of fishing.

Rainbows and browns like to congregate off river mouths, drop-offs, points, submerged islands and sandbars, and other types of lake structures that feature deep water close to shore. Wading is often the most productive method of fishing early in the year. I feel the months of April through June are the best times to go after both species of trout.

My technique for wading is to work into thigh- or hip-deep water and make six to twelve casts in a semicircle in front of me and then to shuffle slowly down the shoreline for about thirty feet and resume casting. Early in the year the fish are generally close to the surface and many times the distinct swirl or splash of a feeding trout can pinpoint their location.

Experimentation with lure sinking time and retrieves is important because trout in lakes are finicky. They have time to critically analyze the lure, and if everything doesn't look kosher they'll ignore it or spook into deep water.

Many times I've run into the situation with lake rainbows and browns where a spoon just doesn't turn them on. They want something different; in this case I usually resort to a Notangle Spinner and fish slow and deep with a spinner blade that barely turns over.

The smaller 1/8- and 1/4-ounce spinners seem to be much more productive for inland lake trout fishing than the 1/2-ounce size. My most productive colors have been nickel, nickel and blue, copper, hammered nickel and blue, and nickel inside with an orange and green perch scale. Not too many people know it, but perch (small ones) are a preferred food source for rainbows and browns in many inland lakes.

The spinner should be cast out and retrieved just as slowly as possible while still bringing out the throbbing action of the blade. These trout often strike hard, and you have little trouble telling you've had a strike. The bigger ones hit, sizzle off up to fifty yards of line on the strike, and then resort to a series of head-shaking jumps and cartwheels.

River fishing is one area where the Notangle Spinner holds its own against any other lure. I've taken countless 'bows and brown on this lure and have often seen it outproduce other lures three to one.

The primary necessity in river fishing is to determine where browns and rainbows will be found. They tend to frequent entirely different locations. Rainbows often are found in heavier current than browns; the tail end of a hole is prime location to begin your search. Another hot spot

*George Richey picked up this lunker brown by wading the shallows of Lake Michigan and casting Devle Dogs.*

*George Richey gilling a big brown.*

for rainbows, especially during hot weather, is in shallow, fast riffles where the water is highly oxygenated.

Browns, on the other hand, are usually found in slower, deeper water. Deep runs along the riverbanks, pockets of deep water, and slow, still pools often hold big browns.

If I'm fishing a river for rainbows I'll normally concentrate my efforts in the tail end of a pool, that area where the water quickens up before spilling over into the next riffle. Cast a Notangle Spinner or Dardevle Spinnie across and upstream and allow it to sink on a tight line. As the lure or spinner begins bumping along bottom, keep the rod tip fairly high and ease it over underwater obstructions. Reel just fast enough to bring out the wobble of the spoon or the throbbing beat of the spinner blade.

As the lure straightens out below you, bob it once or twice in the current and reel it back fast. The rainbow will generally strike as the lure swings around downstream on a tight line.

Another technique is to cast directly upstream and retrieve the lure right along the bottom. Most stream trout will be holding directly on bottom, and it pays to get your lure down to the required depth.

One of the best techniques I've learned for river browns is to work the deep-water edges of riverbanks or deep holes and runs. Browns take refuge under or near submerged brush or roots in many streams. A small spoon or spinner, on fairly light line, worked down to the fish can be a dynamite method of fishing.

*Small creeks are superb places to find big browns during fall months.*

Some experts I know fish browns with Notangle Spinners by wading upstream slowly and spotcasting lures to any logjam, deep hole or other possible hiding place. They probe casts everywhere. This method of fishing works wonders in locating foraging fish.

A book of this type wouldn't be complete without mentioning the fact that some of the largest river browns are taken by fishing after dark. I suggest wading down through a stretch of river during daylight hours and sizing up the water and possible holding spots.

When darkness is complete I like to begin fishing in a slow, methodical manner. Never rush your casts; fish each one out thoroughly because after-dark browns often follow a lure up to a motionless fisherman and strike right at the rod tip.

Larger lures like the Dardevlet, Dardevle Imp, Cop-E-Cat Imp and Devle Dog work exceptionally well once the sun goes down. I like darker lures which are silhouetted against the night sky. I feel big browns can spot them easier. I lean toward copper, black and white chunk, crackle frog with a copper inside, or blue. Nickel-colored spoons pay off at various times, and it's worthwhile to have a good selection in your creel.

Browns can often be heard feeding after dark, so I always listen for the sounds of slurping fish. If you hear a fish, begin fishing for that fish until he either stops feeding or strikes.

If the night sounds on the river are quiet, begin a systematic combing of the entire river. Pay particular attention to the banks, any overhanging brush or tree, logjams, or relatively shallow stretches of flat water. Browns often move into the flats under cover of darkness to feed.

Cast across and downstream and allow the spoon to wobble and tumble as it swings across on a tight line. Most strikes will occur as the line straightens out below you. If a fish doesn't strike as the lure swings across the current, jiggle the lure a couple of times as it hangs motionless below you in the current; then retrieve it slowly. I've had browns peck away at the spoon as I was bringing it in and finally grab it within inches of the rod. On a dark night, that amounts to a thrill beyond compare.

I've taken a few river browns after dark by casting a spoon directly upstream into the head of a deep hole and then retrieving it just fast enough to bring out the side-to-side wobble. This can be a deadly method of fishing larger deep holes.

Lake fishing for browns and rainbows can be either an exceedingly enjoyable pastime or a waste of time providing few fish. The key lies in knowing how to fish. Trolling is the most successful tactic with these fish.

I've fished the Great Lakes for years for the jumbo fish found in Lakes

*Trolling small Dardevles in inland lakes is a good method for catching rainbow trout.*

Michigan and Huron. This is a predictable fishery during spring and early summer months. A productive method is to longline the shallow water for these fish. We use six-pound monofilament and either spinning or baitcasting outfits. A Devle Dog in silver, silver and blue, or pearl is attached to the line with the smallest snap available. We initially release anywhere from 125 to 150 yards of line from a slow-moving small boat. These lures will sink about five feet on a slow troll, and it's important to adjust the trolling speed to bring out the optimum action.

The best locations for trolling are off deepwater points, river mouths, gravel bars, deep drop-offs close to shore, and sunken islands or sandbars. Browns work into these areas to feed on the available forage fish. The months of May and June are best.

Browns often cruise just under the surface and will explode in a shower of spray as they herd minnows towards each other. The sight of a school of fifty to a hundred browns committing mayhem on minnows has to be seen to be appreciated. This rolling, porpoising action can be seen for a mile or more under ideal conditions. Some fishermen scan the horizon with binoculars to locate schools of feeding fish.

Once a school is located, it is best to troll around the outside edges rather than work directly through the pod of fish. Enough fish will be exposed to the action of the spoon to provide top-flight sport.

The best fishing normally occurs right at daybreak, but I've had peak action on blistering hot days under a cloudless sky. The important thing is to locate the fish, and sometimes this will take the better part of the day.

I've stated that it requires a long, fine line to interest lake browns in striking. It also helps to steer a zigzag course and weave from shallow water to deep and back again. Short, sudden bursts of speed often create the impression that the spoon is trying to get away. Browns often follow lures for some distance without striking, and this trick will often convert a following fish into a landed trophy.

Rainbows and browns are found throughout North America, but several locations are known worldwide as *the* places to go for top-quality fishing. In the Midwest I highly recommend lakes Michigan and Huron, as well as Lake Superior, as producing some of the best fishing I've ever experienced. Both Michigan and Wisconsin waters are highly rated.

Tennessee offers good fishing for rainbows and browns in Dale Hollow. I'd highly recommend Star Point Lodge near Byrdstown as a good starting point.

Several water reservoirs comprising the New York City supply system, such as Pepacton and Ashokan, offer good trout fishing. Many of these reservoirs do not allow motors for trolling.

*A Dardevle Skeeter on a flyrod can be deadly medicine for rainbows in a stream.*

An underfished brown trout fishery exists along secluded portions of Ontario's Georgian Bay waters. River mouths entering Lake Huron or Georgian Bay offer first-class brown and rainbow fishing.

One of the brightest spots on the brown trout scene is Utah's famous

*The author's father, Lawrence Richey, shows off a nice rainbow which struck a Cop-E-Cat Imp trolled behind a set of Cowbells.*

Flaming Gorge Reservoir. This lake is currently producing browns of world-record size. The North American brown trout record came from this lake (although that record is currently being reviewed).

Rainbows and browns are found throughout the country, but some of the finest fishing for these species can be found in mountain streams of the southeast. Tennessee, Georgia, North and South Carolina, and West Virginia have excellent fishing in streams seldom visited by local anglers.

Montana has some excellent rainbow and brown trout fishing in the Missouri, Gallatin, Madison, Big Hole and Yellowstone rivers.

Wyoming offers excellent fishing in Ross Lake, Hidden Lake, the lower Little Popo Agie River, as well as most of the streams and some lakes in Yellowstone Park.

The Finger Lakes region of New York offers good rainbow trout fishing during spring months. Good brown trout fishing can be had in the Battenkill, Delaware, Beverkill, Upper Hudson and Willowemoc rivers, although portions of these streams are "flies only."

Pennsylvania has brown and rainbow trout in quantity in streams such as the Allegheny, Big Pine Creek, Kettle Creek, Big Fishing Creek, and in Koon Lake near Centerville. Many streams in the south central region contain trout, although many rivers are for fly fishing only.

The White River below Bull Shoals Lake in Arkansas is considered one of the finest streams in the nation for rainbows and browns.

Rainbow and brown trout fishing is a way of life for many North American anglers, and we're fortunate to have Dardevle lures with which to pursue our sport. They shorten the time between strikes and help us enjoy better trout fishing.

# *Lake Trout Are Suckers for Dardevles*

Greg Meadows of California and I were easing along a rocky crag on Great Bear Lake in the Northwest Territories. Our Indian guide, Charley Hamelin from Bransons Lodge, had told us that large schools of lunker lake trout frequented the cove we were trolling. "Big fish!" he'd muttered.

We rounded a small point in the cove, and Greg's spinning rod buckled toward the water. He set the hook, reeled quickly to take up slack line, and struck again with a one-two jab.

Thirty yards behind the boat a huge lake trout coasted to the surface, apparently disliking what he saw, and headed for the bottom in a sizzling sprint that had Greg's reel smoking. Charley backed up the boat so Greg would be directly over the fish, and the battle seesawed back and forth for a half hour before Greg could see the fish rolling and twisting twenty feet below the boat.

"He's big!" Greg hollered. The fish would surface, just out of netting range, and then submarine for bottom again. Slowly the rod took the starch from the fish and it rolled to the surface. Charley expertly slid the net under a fork-tailed trout. When we weighed it later, the fish scaled twenty-four pounds.

Two hours after Greg landed his prize, I set the hooks of my yellow-with-five-red-diamonds Rok't Devle into the jaws of something that didn't like it. My reel was stocked with 250 yards of fifteen-pound mono, and the fish took nearly all of it before we could get the boat turned around. The laker headed out over very deep water and apparently dove for bottom, far below.

We hovered over the fish; and I'd pump and reel, pump and reel; and slowly the trout eased closer to the surface. I spotted it once, about thirty feet down, and it appeared to be well over fifty pounds.

I wanted that fish so badly I could taste it, but it wasn't meant to be.

*The author poses with a twenty-six-pound lake trout taken from Bransons Lodge on Great Bear Lake in the Northwest Territories.*

We struggled back and forth over fifty yards of line for another fifteen minutes, and it appeared to be a Mexican standoff: the fish wouldn't be pressured any further and I found it impossible to move him. Finally, after a lengthy battle, my line broke with a ping and the trout slowly faded into deep water.

Great Bear Lake, and Bransons Lodge, is located right on the Arctic Circle. This is the most fantastic lake trout fishing hole on the North American continent. Bransons boasts the world record lake trout after a customer boated a sixty-five-pounder. Fish of forty to fifty pounds are taken yearly from this huge aquarium-like lake.

It's not unusual to catch and release thirty or more lake trout daily from Great Bear. Not all fish will be in the trophy class, but enough fish from twenty to thirty pounds are taken by avid fishermen to satisfy anyone's needs. Most camps like Bransons advocate a policy of each angler taking home one trophy fish and making up the balance of his limit with smaller eight-to-twelve-pounders.

These smaller fish are abundant. It's not unusual to locate schools of small lakers in shallow water, and they'll all compete for a Dardevle cast in their direction. It's the thrill of a lifetime to whang out a spoon and watch forty or fifty fish peel toward it.

It's been said by many fishermen that any lure could catch lake trout at Bransons, but this is only partly true. In years past I've caught Canadian lakers on bent tablespoons with a treble hook attached or on a bare hook with red yarn or flannel attached. But for consistent catches of bigger fish it takes a lure like the Dardevle with its built-in action.

Two specific techniques have proven successful on my trips to Great Bear Lake. The first, and easiest, is to troll slowly around shallower bays in the lake. Lakers in Great Bear are normally found close to the surface; you'll seldom need any weight to get down to them.

I'll usually cast a red-with-white-stripe or yellow-with-five-red-diamonds Dardevle, Rok't Devle, Seadevlet or Cop-E-Cat Jr. about twenty or thirty yards behind the boat. A putt-putt slow trolling speed is used, and the spoon sinks only five or six feet at the proper speeds.

As I troll, I give the rod tip a sharp jerk or two to increase the lure's action. This "chugging" technique often results in a heavy strike. The fish generally strike as the lure settles back into its normal wobble.

*Greg Meadows gills a big laker into the boat on Great Bear Lake.*

Whenever we'd enter a very shallow bay where the water was less than ten or fifteen feet deep it was possible to locate schools of smaller lake trout which were always willing to bite. We'd coast to a stop, turn off the engines, and drift slowly with the wind, casting toward visible schools of trout.

Contrary to popular opinion, it doesn't take an extremely large lure to sucker lake trout in Great Bear. Much of my casting is done with Dardevlets, Dardevle Imp, and Dardevlet Klickers. All nickel, red with white stripe, and chartreuse with red spots seemed to be the best colors.

I'd cast near the schools of lake trout and begin a frantic retrieve,

*Meadows with another whopper lake trout taken at Bransons Lodge.*

trying to make the lure look like it was trying to outrun the fish. It's impossible to reel too fast when a laker turns on the afterburners and decides he wants the lure. It's no contest as the strike turns into a slam-bang affair.

Great Bear Lake has huge boulders jutting up from bottom, and although Dardevle's hooks are of the best steel and are sharp when they come from the factory, it doesn't take too long before the hook points become dull. I carry a small file and touch up the hooks once in a while. My points are needle sharp, and when I set the hooks the result is generally a well-hooked laker.

Whenever I cast for the smaller lakers I usually pinch down the hook barbs so that the hooks can be removed easily without lifting the fish into the boat.

The vast sprawling lakes of the Northwest Territories aren't the only places to do battle with big lake trout. An energetic planting program in the Great Lakes during the mid-1960s has paved the way for good lake trout fishing closer to home for many anglers.

Midwest states such as Michigan, Wisconsin, Indiana, Illinois and Minnesota are currently stocking or have stocked good numbers of lakers in Lakes Superior, Michigan and Huron. Some lake trout are showing up in fish boxes in Lakes Erie and Ontario but not in the numbers taken in the three upper Great Lakes.

Lake trout fishing in the Great Lakes can be a year-round affair; ice fishermen consider jigging in deep water during winter months the height of fun.

*When lake trout activity reaches a feverish pitch in the Great Lakes, action like this can be encountered.*

Lakers commonly move into shoal water in April, May or June, depending on the area and water temperature. Fishing often takes place in fifteen to thirty-five feet of water at this time.

As summer heat warms the water and forage fish move into deeper areas the lake trout follow suit, so summer fishing may take place depths as great as 150 feet, depending on water temperature. Lakers seem to prefer a water temperature of about forty-eight to fifty degrees.

As fall winds begin blowing and the water cools off, lake trout again make an inshore migration for spawning purposes. They'll often be caught during October and November in six to fifteen feet of water, usually over submerged rocks, gravel bars or riprap.

Night fishing is a popular method of catching fall lake trout. The fisherman wades in knee-deep water and casts a fan-shaped pattern in front of him as he moves slowly down the lake. I like to cast a half dozen times, move down about twenty yards, and cast again.

The Devle Dog or Devle Dog Jr. in nickel with black and white stripe, nickel back with red and white stripe, all nickel, pearl, or nickel back with half-nickel–half-blue have been my most consistent producers.

Cast out, allow the lure to sink slowly on a tight line, and then retrieve it slowly at a speed designed to bring out the best action. An occasional twitch of the rod tip will cause the lure to dart and dive as it is retrieved. Lakers often strike the spoon as it hits the water, or as it sinks, and you have to be alert to this possibility. I set the hook anytime the lure feels different. Many times it will just be ticking over the rocks, but occasionally a fish will have it.

Spring trolling is a major Great Lakes sport, and few fishermen realize that lakers are often found in the upper ten feet of water for about a month after ice-out. I like to troll a fairly long line (about fifty yards) behind the boat and select a Dardevle of a size and shape comparable to the alewives and smelt the trout are feeding on. For this type of fishing a Dardevle Imp, Thindevle, Cop-E-Cat Imp or Dardevlet Klicker gets the nod. The all nickel, nickel and blue, nickel back with chartreuse and red spots, or nickel back with blue herring scale would be my choices. The shad (alewife) color is also very good at times.

I seldom attach larger than a half-ounce or one-ounce sinker to my fishing line. I place it two or three feet ahead of the spoon, and it helps overcome the long lines and the trolling speed of the boat.

You can fish either with a hand-held rod or with the lines attached to outriggers to hold them away from the boat. Short, quick turns to port or starboard will cause the lures to dart one way and then the other. Lakers are great followers of lures, and this technique often proves to be their undoing.

Once lakers go deep, usually in June or July, fishing takes on another entirely different aspect. Summer lake trout fishing, with downriggers, will be covered in another chapter.

One of the most successful methods of deep fishing that I've used is to troll with monofilament line testing about fifteen pounds. The line from the rod goes down to a three-way swivel. A dropper line extends off the bottom swivel, and anywhere from six to twelve ounces of lead is used, depending on the depth of water being fished.

An eighteen-to-twenty-four-inch leader is tied to the third eye of the swivel and to a sturdy snap swivel. Now comes the clincher: I use either a Thindevle, Jr. Flutter Devle or King Flutter Devle. These thinner spoons are easily activated by the fisherman using this "chugging" technique. Nickel and blue, all nickel, and pearl are the most productive colors and thus my favorites.

A slow trolling speed is very important when fishing deep water. You must be able to accurately feel the bottom. Lakers are pretty much bottom-oriented most (not all) of the time.

The weight and spoon are lowered slowly to bottom. Keep finger or thumb pressure on the spool to prevent overrun. Once the weight bumps bottom, put the spool into gear and slowly "chug" (lift the rod tip to a vertical position followed by a rapid lowering to a horizontal position). If you can feel the weight bump bottom again, you're in business.

If you can't feel bottom, release more line until you strike bottom again. This time you should be effectively fishing at the proper depth. I've found that a chugging movement of the rod tip every five or ten seconds is essential to success.

Lake trout usually strike either as the rod tip is lifted to the vertical position or as the rod is lowered. As the rod tip is lowered to near the surface, the lure will flutter downward like an injured minnow and the strikes can be ferocious. I know more than one man who has suffered a sprained wrist during a savage lake trout strike.

Another trick many fishermen have learned to incorporate with lake trout chugging is to give the motor a ten-foot burst of speed. This causes the lure to lift off bottom in a frantic upwards dash. Slow the boat down immediately and the lure will wobble downwards in a slow descent. Lakers often strike as the lure speeds up or just after it settles to the bottom.

Once I was fishing Manitoba's Lake Athapapuskow for lake trout, and the fishing was slow; in fact, it was dead. We trolled, and then we cast Dardevles in likely areas, but nothing worked.

We finally decided to try jigging. It was the only tactic we hadn't tried, and at this stage of the game we were ready for anything.

We drifted into a deep cove and lowered a hammered nickel Huskie Devle and Jr. Huskie Devle into the depths. It seemed to take a minute or more for the lures to find bottom.

As they touched down we began a vigorous up-and-down jigging movement. I felt something tick my spoon. It could have been a rock, but just in case I started cranking the spinning reel handle rapidly. A lake trout nailed the lure before it had traveled ten feet. I jabbed the hooks home twice and held on as the fish headed downlake.

My buddy tried the same trick and was immediately into a big fish. His trout went one way while mine ran the other. We fought that team of lakers for twenty minutes before my twenty-two-pounder was safely in the net. Bill, his rod bowed double, held on for almost forty minutes before we managed to gaff a thirty-four-pounder through the bottom jaw and lift him into the boat. Our zero day had suddenly risen in our estimation to a dream trip.

Jigging can be accomplished in many ways, and the Dardevle brand of lures is well-suited to all methods of jigging. Another technique which has proven successful for Ontario lakers is to cast the lure out, allow it to settle to bottom, jig it once or twice and reel it back to the boat in slow combinations of jigs and retrieves.

I've taken lakers from swift subarctic rivers, where spot-casting Dardevles to boulders and to the pockets of quiet water behind them will produce fast-paced action for fish in the five-to-fifteen-pound class. The fish are accustomed to eating anything that the river carries down to them, and few fish can refuse the seductive wobble of a well-placed Dardevle.

Lake trout are found all over North America, from the high subarctic lakes like Great Bear to remote high mountain lakes in the Rockies. In between are the laker-rich waters of the Great Lakes.

Some of the finest trophy lake trout in recent years have come from the Canadian provinces. Great Bear Lake and Great Slave Lake in the Northwest Territories are two prime examples of excellent lake trout waters.

Lake Athabasca, Reindeer Lake and Wolleston Lake are three excellent lakes in Saskatchewan.

Gods Lake in Manitoba has produced many exceptional lake trout in recent years and is a very good choice for big fish. Lake Athapapuskow, near Flin Flon, is a drive-in lake where big trout are caught.

Lake trout have been planted in quite a few high mountain lakes in Montana, Wyoming, Colorado, Utah and California. These fish, known locally as mackinaws, have filled an important niche in many western trout lakes.

The Great Lakes, especially along the shorelines of Michigan, Illinois, Indiana and Wisconsin, are currently producing large numbers of lake trout ranging from three to twenty pounds.

Lakers are found in a few scattered lakes in New York and Pennsylvania as well as in Maine.

## *The Spinner and the Steelhead*

Seldom do new techniques evolve that will consistently take big fish. But last year I stumbled on a trick that will take steelhead anywhere they exist, whether in Michigan, Wisconsin, Ontario, Minnesota or the steelhead-rich West Coast states and provinces.

To briefly illustrate how this technique works let's review a guide trip I once had in which my client and I hooked twenty-three steelhead in one day.

I was guiding a customer on Michigan's Betsie River. We walked the riverbank slowly and moved upstream. Slow, cautious steps kept the steelhead from being spooked off their shallow spawning beds. The river was three feet deep and as clear as distilled water.

We'd covered about two hundred yards when we found a small patch of gravel the size of an average living room. The current flowed swiftly and heavily over the bar. As we approached I could see the flashing sides of a spawning steelhead; her flanks glinted in the weak sunlight as she dug the redd with her tail. Holding nearby were five male fish, resplendent in their pinkish-orange spawning colors and as eager as young beavers.

One male fish was well over fifteen pounds in weight. The smallest fish weighed about ten pounds. My customer was excited and I had to warn him against making too much noise or any sudden movements.

Polarized sunglasses helped cut the glare and enabled us to spot the motionless fish. Without them, the steelhead would have looked like logs or shadows on the bottom.

"Where do you want me?" he asked. I slowly led him downstream to a spot where we could enter the river thirty yards below the fish. We cautiously worked upstream until we were about ten yards from the spawning steelhead.

*Gordie Fawcett of Minnesota did well fishing with the author on Notangle Spinners on a Michigan stream.*

*The author gills a big steelhead on a western river. It struck a silver Notangle Spinner fished deep through a hole.*

"Stand with your back against that willow tree," I told him. "It'll help break up your silhouette and will keep your rod movements hidden from the fish."

Once we were in good casting position I knotted a copper bladed Notangle Spinner onto his fifteen-pound monofilament. "That's a new kind of spinner to me," he said. "It's not so new," I commented. "They've been around for many years. Its just that many people have never seen one. I like 'em because they don't twist your line like other spinners and they catch steelhead."

The steelhead were restless in their eagerness to begin spawning. The males would dart in and out of the redd while the female continued to put the finishing touches on the spawning site.

"Whatever you do, don't hook the female. As long as she isn't hooked or unduly disturbed the males will keep coming back to her," I said. If a female is hooked and then regains her freedom she'll leave the area and take any male fish with her. I've seen as many as six bucks caught off one spawning bed when the female remains unhooked.

His first cast was a bit wild due to the excitement of casting to big fish. I slowed him down and told him to place the spinner six to ten feet upstream from the fish. I advised him to reel just fast enough to keep the line tight and to keep the spinner blade turning over as the spinner tumbled downstream. The blade has to be revolving as it passes the fish to ensure a strike.

His next cast was perfect, and the biggest male grabbed the Notangle Spinner as it drifted through the bed. "Set the hook!" I yelled, but the fish dropped it without being hooked.

"You've got him interested," I said. "Keep casting to the same spot." His next four casts landed in the magic spot, and the big pink-sided male responded by following the spinner from the bed on each cast. "Keep working him," I said. Teasing spawning steelhead calls for an iron wrist and grim determination to keep placing the spinner in the same spot time after time. Repetitious accurate casting is the key to this type of fishing.

The next cast resulted in a savage strike as the steelhead grabbed the spinner and tore off upstream with his back out of water. Thirty yards upstream he splashed into the air, the Notangle Spinner dangling from his upper jaw.

We waded into the river and my client kept the pressure on, forcing the fish to fight the rod and the current. Twice the fish drifted with the current downstream toward us but managed to evade my net. After a fifteen-minute seesaw battle the fish was tired out and I was able to scoop up a 16½-pound steelhead, the man's first big steelhead and his first trophy from any river.

The remainder of the day was a repetition of the foregoing action as we battled trout after trout. Twenty-three steelhead were hooked, including three fish weighing over twenty pounds. We didn't land most of them due to the narrow, brush-chocked, logjammed stream, but we were able to win over two besides the first: a fifteen-pounder and a smaller 10½-pound fish.

I've fished steelhead for twenty-five years and have taken well over

*These boat fishermen hooked a nice steelhead ahead of this logjam.*

*These fishermen combined forces to land a big steelhead that struck a copper Notangle Spinner.*

*Action! That's what steelhead fishing is all about.*

three thousand fish, but this method of taking big fish is the most action-packed way I've discovered. The amazing fact about this fishing technique is that very few small steelhead are caught. Where I fish, anything under ten pounds is considered small.

The primary factor is making this system productive is fishing on a clear, relatively shallow stream. The river shouldn't be over four feet deep and you should look for bottom consisting of marble-sized gravel, the ideal size for spawning steelhead. A fisherman should walk upstream along the riverbank (stay out of water unless actually casting to fish), stop often, and look a lot. It's like stillhunting deer; walk a little and then sift the water apart for signs of fish. A downstream riverbank approach is often possible, although the fish will generally spot the angler before he spots them.

Once fish are located, two approaches pay off. The downstream approach with an upstream cast has already been discussed. The upstream approach puts the angler above the fish. This often provides easier angling, but the possibility of spooking the fish is much greater. It takes a person with the stealth of a cat burglar to work within casting distance of steelhead from an upstream position. Slow, deliberate movements, no splashy steps and a minimum of rod movement are needed to take steelhead this way.

Approach the spawning bed from upstream and try to keep at least twenty yards between you and the fish. If they begin darting around and

*This fisherman just hooked a big steelhead on a Notangle Spinner and is heading downstream.*

appear extremely restless, stop moving and remain motionless until they calm down. If the fish spook, get into casting position while they are gone and remain motionless until they return and resume spawning.

Cast the spinner so it will alight to one side of the male fish and allow the current to swing the lure by his nose. A split shot or two is often necessary to keep the spinner skimming just over the gravel bottom.

Whenever the spinner stops, even if you don't see the strike, set the hook. I always fish for the trout's nose; and if I see it move, even an inch, when the spinner is near I'll set the hook hard. Steelhead can literally suck in a spinner from as much as six inches away without appearing to move. Strikes are usually a soft take, although occasionally a big buck will really hammer the spinner.

I've found most of my steelhead are caught on 1/8- and 1/4-ounce Notangle Spinners with copper blades. Silver, brass, or red and white spinner blades also work. On occasion, when the fish are frightened from the flash of a bright spinner, I'll resort to using a home-painted all-black spinner blade.

Steelhead fishing is one of the top sports in many areas and I'm grateful for the Notangle Spinner. Without it I'm afraid I wouldn't be able to land as many steelhead as I do.

# Largemouth and Smallmouth Bass

Largemouth and smallmouth bass are prized gamefish which offer a wide variety of life styles. The largemouth bass is at home in warmer lakes dotted with emergent aquatic vegetation such as lily pads or deep weed beds, swimming rafts, drowned timber and hyacinths. The smallmouth bass lives in either lakes or streams but he likes colder water. Largemouth bass like a water temperature of 70–72°F., while smallmouth bass prefer 65–68 degrees. Clear, deep lakes or swift streams are the type of habitat the smallmouth prefers. He favors rubble, boulders, reed beds, sharp drop-offs, points or any place where a cool clear river flows into the lake.

One of the best techniques I've seen for taking big bass was shown to me on California's Lake Miramar. This jumbo-bass lake is crawling with

Tom Huggler works a Weedless Dardevlet from this largemouth's jaw.

*A water thermometer makes bass fishing easy.*

fish of eight to twelve pounds, some larger. The occasional fish will push the fifteen-to-eighteen-pound mark.

We anchored and began bottom crawling Dardevles off the rocky shorelines. Rocky points have always produced some of the biggest largemouth bass of my career. We'd cast out, let the spoons settle to the bottom, and bring 'em back slowly enough to occasionally get tangled with bottom; but the slow Dardevle wobble drove those bass nuts.

Big bass are usually a hit-or-miss affair and our action lasted only about an hour, but we hung several fish of trophy proportions. My buddy managed to subdue a thirteen-pounder, our largest, but the hawg bass seemed to be concentrated in one small area.

I like to fish small, isolated coves in wee lakes for big largemouth and cast along partially submerged logs, deep edges of weed beds or alongside lily pads. Bass are used to grabbing huge mouthfuls of baitfish when they go on the prowl, so I often use a Huskie Jr.

Southern largemouth bass, during late winter and early spring months, often go on the prowl just before spawning begins. I've had some excellent bass fishing by cruising and spot-casting Dardevles to likely looking hummocks, beneath cypress knees or alongside clumps of hyacinths.

Once I was fishing the Suwannee River and neighboring bayous in Georgia's Okefenokee Swamp. We drifted along, quietly sculling a canoe paddle, pegging accurate casts beneath the overhanging Spanish moss and dropping red-and-white or black-and-yellow Dardevles along the cypress stumps.

Many of the largemouth bass were in the two-to-three-pound class and would smack the lure as if they weighed ten times as much. We pushed through the cobwebs spanning narrow openings and worked deeper into the swamp; the further back in we went, the more action we found.

After two hours of doing battle with smaller bass I slammed the hooks home into a wildly spinning, tailwalking largemouth that shattered the peaceful silence of the swamp. The fish danced an acrobatic jig for quite a spell before I managed to grab its lower jaw and lift a pot-bellied seven-pound female into the canoe.

My buddy followed shortly with a 7½-pounder that jumped on a copper-colored Dardevlet. The cast was a mite too long and landed on a twig about a foot above the water. He jiggled his rod tip several times and the spoon dropped into the water at the base of the stump. A largemouth pounced on the lure like a cat on a mouse, and water sprayed in all directions as he slapped the water apart with his tail and headed for home with his prize. My buddy set the hooks and held on strongly as the fish tried to burrow under the cypress stump. After a short battle we slid the fish into the canoe, and my trip to Okenfenokee was history.

This same fishing technique works well all through the south where bass grow big and mean in an environment that taxes an angler's casting and fishing skills.

My fishing buddy Al Eason, a fishing guide from Overton, Texas, is a firm believer in Dardevle lures and their ability to produce bass. Al guides on Caddo Lake on the Texas–Louisiana border and he believes in giving all sizes of Dardevles a good fishing. He likes to watch the large gulls that work the lake during the fall months. These birds often give an angler a clue to schools of bass which are feeding in the area. Al likes to fish deep, with fairly light line; the bass often pick up the spoon as it sinks into about forty-five feet of water.

Another trick he likes to use is to watch the lake's surface (when it's calm) for signs of bass chasing minnows on top. Small Dardevle Imps and Devle Dogs, skittered on the surface, will often result in a quick limit of schooling bass.

In southern impoundments, Weedless Dardevles wormed and twisted through dead and drowned tree branches provide a fisherman with top-quality action.

Bottom nudging is a technique I've used in various impoundments when fishing gets slow. I select a deepwater point area, move in, and cut

*Casting is my favorite method of working various largemouth and smallmouth bass hotspots on a lake.*

my Evinrude engine. I lower a Dardevle over the gunwale and spool it slowly to bottom. As my Lund boat is caught by the wind and begins a slow drift out into deep water, I release additional line so the lure will hover close to bottom. The object is to creep the spoon over the bottom and give it an occasional upward jig for six inches to a foot. This adds lure motion and sends off sound waves which a feeding bass can home in to.

This trick worked well for me one time on Bull Shoals in northern

Arkansas. It's a technique worth remembering when bass are deep during midsummer and reluctant to strike other, normal retrieves.

One thing many newcomers to bass fishing fail to realize is that bass dislike direct sunlight. Knowledge of this fact can often help you take a bass from the dark side of any structure. I've taken good catches of bass from such impoundments as Toledo Bend and Sam Rayburn in Texas, and from Eufaula and Tenkiller Reservoirs in Oklahoma, by fishing the dark sides of old roadbeds, creek beds, roadside ditches and even graveyards. It gives one a ghostly feeling to drop a Dardevle into an abandoned, water-filled gravesite, but largemouth bass like such areas.

I've had excellent bass fishing in many northern lakes with Dardevles. I used to live in southern Michigan, and Lake Fenton was a goldmine for big largemouths. Daytime fishermen seldom caught the fish; it was the after-dark hombre that took home his limit of lunkers.

My strategy was to slowly row around the lake and spot-cast a Dardevle (black and white chunk) against the shoreline and retrieve slowly without any extra action. The strikes usually occurred just after the lure splashed into the water or just after it passed over the edge of the dropoff.

Favorite spots to look for cruising largemouth were along the edges of lily pads, boat ramps, swimming beaches, rafts, and docks, or wherever brush or heavy weeds were found in the shallows. This type of fishing demanded accurate casting and no lights. The use of any lights would send the bass scurrying for the depths. My biggest bass weighed just over seven pounds and provided me with all the action I could handle without benefit of a light. Once he was in the boat, I stuck the oars in the water and rowed for shore to weigh him. It was a thrill I'll never forget.

Fishing for smallmouth bass is another story. These fish are found in wilder places—far northern lakes and streams where pollution and man haven't made their presence felt. The smallmouth is the hard-rock scrapper with red in his eye and a mean, evil disposition. He shares his water with northern pike and walleye, and a fish has to have a mean streak in him to compete and survive against those two vicious predators.

Years ago I lucked onto a technique for taking big smallmouth bass. I was casting black and white chunk Dardevlets in Michigan's Manistee Lake for walleyes. It was August, a hot night, and the walleye action came and went; we caught several fish in the six-to-eight-pound class.

As the full moon came up I kept casting to the points and drop-offs for walleye, but the smallmouth showed up and the walleyes moved elsewhere. The spoon would land with a healthy splash visible by the

*Jumbo smallmouth bass like this five-pounder can easily inhale a good sized Dardevle.*

*Smallmouth like this chunky catch is enough to make any kid happy.*

moonbeams playing on the water, and we'd take only two or three cranks on the reel handle before the first smallmouth hit.

It was a savage strike and was followed instantly by a crashing jump. "That's no walleye!" I said, as the fish went berserk. I played the smallie for several minutes before sliding him—a six-pounder—into the net.

We caught four more smallmouth in the four-to-five-pound range before the action petered out. Every fish would strike either near shore or just as the spoon slid over the drop-off and into deeper water. The black and white coloration of the lure was silhouetted against the night sky and made it easy for the bass to zero in on a supposedly easy meal.

Another time I was pounding a rocky reef in eight feet of water in Ontario's Lake of the Woods near Kenora. I'd seen smallmouth bass taken off this reef during an earlier visit and went back loaded with Dardevles to prospect.

I anchored in deeper water just off the edge of the reef and began casting Dardevle Imps and Dardevle Spinnies onto the reef and simply edging 'em back slowly. The smallmouths would pounce from behind a boulder and smack the lure as it wobbled by. As soon as one reef would play out I'd up the anchor and hop to another reef or point, or to the edge of a reed bed or island, and find hot action again.

Smallmouth are willing biters, but many fishermen decrease their chances by fishing with too-heavy line. When I'm specifically going after smallmouths I seldom use over six-pound monofilament. The smaller diameter line makes for easier casts and more strikes.

Dale Hollow Lake on the Tennessee–Kentucky border has some whopper smallmouths available, and one of the methods I've used in the past is to try jigging deep water with smaller-sized Dardevles. The Devle Dog Jr. and Dardevle Spinnie have made good jigging lures when I've fished out of Star Point near Byrdstown, Tennessee.

I'll locate an area where I feel smallmouths should be located, such as off a steep bank, drop-off, or point, and slowly wind-drift along the drop-off with a steady jugging movement. The bass are usually found feeding near bottom, and this wind-drift jigging technique is a good one with which to locate them.

Once the fish were found I preferred to anchor slightly upwind and probe the depths with various colors and sizes of Dardevles to determine which lure, color, and retrieve combination was most productive. Two or three times I've been able to make limit catches of big smallmouth by first locating the fish and then by anchoring and casting.

A shore-fishing technique that works well is to find a drop-off near a point and cast medium-sized Dardevles out into deep water. Allow the spoons to sink to various depths and then inch the lure up the ledge near shore. Smallmouths often lie along the edge of a drop-off, near bottom, and ambush a lure as it creeps nose-first up the drop-off. This method has worked very well for me in many Canadian lakes.

Stream fishing for smallmouths is another story. The fish are usually concentrated in deeper holes along the outside of the riverbank, and it takes pinpoint accuracy as well as a wide repertoire of retrieves to consistently take fish in moving water.

Many Canadian and northern U.S. streams have smallmouth bass. Although they seldom average as large as lake fish, they more than make up for their size by using the water current in a fight against the angler and his rod.

Avoid silhouetting yourself against the sky when approaching stream smallies. I like to approach a stream hole with some type of cover behind me to break up my outline.

I use smaller lures like the Dardevle Spinnie and Dardevle Midget when fishing streams. I normally use bright colors on dull, overcast days and duller spoons on bright days.

A cast quartering across and upstream and retrieved just off bottom has been my most successful river fishing technique. The lure should work close to the riverbank, through the tail ends of riffles and through any deep pocket of cover. Smallmouth often hole up in front of, behind, or alongside submerged brush piles or logjams.

I'll often try to peg casts just as close to brushy cover as possible and feed plenty of slack line so the lure will sink deep and wobble through the best water.

In streams where larger smallmouth exist I'll use a Rok't Devle Imp, a heavier lure which will sink more quickly. This lure enables a fisherman to work deeper water in a more conventional manner without adding any weight to his line.

Smallmouth bass are found throughout the northern tier of states east of the Mississippi and also in Canada. I've encountered good smallmouth fishing in Tennessee, Kentucky, New York, Pennsylvania, Maine, New Hampshire, Vermont, Michigan, Wisconsin, and Minnesota as well as in Ontario and Quebec.

The smallie is a fish worthy of any fisherman's time, and old-timers still believe ounce for ounce that they fight harder than any other species. That's a debate I'll save for the hot stove league, but I'm firmly convinced that they are hard to beat for a savage strike, high acrobatic leaps and bulldog tenacity on the end of your line.

The largemouth bass is more widely distributed than his cousin. Some of my favorite bass fishing states for big fish are Florida, Georgia, Oklahoma, Texas, Ohio, South Carolina, California, Arizona, Louisiana, Tennessee, Missouri, and Arkansas.

# Walleyes and Sauger Go Nuts for Dardevles

Two perennial favorites among fisherman are the walleye and his close cousin, the sauger. Except for minute differences, the two fish are similar in appearance and respond equally well to Dardevle lures.

The sauger's range is quite distinct, and only a mere handful of locations host decent sauger fishing. The sauger inhabits large lakes and river systems and can survive in more turbid waters than the walleye. Walleyes are widely distributed and are found in open lakes and streams. For all practical purposes, techniques that will produce on walleye will work equally well with the closely related but less common sauger.

One of the most pleasurable methods of taking fish is casting, and over the years, I've been able to make limit catches of walleye and sauger by casting various-sized Dardevles.

An example was a fishery on Michigan's Manistee Lake where jumbo walleye used to work into the lake from nearby Lake Michigan via the Big Manistee River. About the first of August, huge numbers of spawning alewives would be finishing up their business and the walleyes would come around to feed on the remnant population of forage fish.

The best fishing occurred on a night with a full moon. We'd move up and down the shoreline from point to point, anchor quietly in deep water, and cast silvery Cop-E-Cat Imps or Dardevlets to the shoreline, exposed pilings, or submerged slab docks. Absolute silence and darkness were essential to success. We fished from a carpeted boat and never used a light when casting or landing fish.

My brother and I eased up to a point, anchored, and began thoroughly working the shallows. After about ten minutes of casting we began hearing a ruckus in the water fifty yards away. "We've found 'em!" George whispered as he slid the anchor up. I began slowly rowing toward the splashing noise.

We anchored again about twenty yards from the surfacing minnows which had been pinned against the shoreline by marauding walleyes. I aimed a cast near shore, and my spoon didn't travel ten feet in the water before it stopped suddenly as if it were hung on bottom. "Got him!" I hissed just as I felt George, too, barb a fish.

My walleye headed for deep water and began the familiar bulldogging battle common to the species. George's fish peeled off his end of the boat in a similar dash for deep water. We quietly and slowly worked the fish from our respective ends of the boat and let the fish fight deeply until it was time to lead them to the net. George's fish tired first and he netted his prize without any noise.

My fish fought longer and harder and refused to come off bottom for a long time. After a fifteen-minute battle he succumbed and came reluctantly to the surface where I netted a fourteen-pound walleye.

George, in the meantime, had unhooked his fish and was tied into

*George Richey poses with a ten-pound walleye which struck a Dardevle fished along the edge of a drop-off.*

another scrappy lunker walleye. His first fish weighed just over ten pounds and was a trophy anyone would be tickled to land.

We pulled three more walleyes from that school before it disappeared into deep water. The smallest fish weighed eight pounds and my lunker was the heaviest. Our five walleyes for the night's fishing weighed a total of fifty-one pounds. Friends, that is superb walleye fishing.

*Harold and Marsha Persails team up on a seven-pound walleye.*

*George Richey and Dave Raskey admire a pair of Manistee Lake (Michigan) walleyes taken after dark.*

Unfortunately, too few fishermen realize that walleyes and sauger are primarily nocturnal feeders. Periods of low light intensity such as overcast days, dusk, dawn, and night are by far the best times to make good catches of these fish.

I prefer to use dark-colored spoons when fishing after dark because I feel the fish can spot them more easily when they are silhouetted against the sky.

Over the years I've made good Dardevle catches of walleye and sauger by fishing drop-offs close to shore. The edge of the drop-off serves as a migration route for cruising fish, and many times they will lie right on bottom and ambush anything which travels near the lake bottom or edge of the drop-off.

I was fishing Kasagami Lake in northern Ontario one time, and my guide told me that a nearby drop-off yielded some of the best walleyes in the lake. Lots of big ones, he claimed. I'd heard the wind blow before but thought I'd give it a try anyway.

We motored three miles to the drop-off and began casting the tea-colored water just before dark. Choosing a yellow-with-red-chunk Dardevle Imp, I cast far out into the lake and began creeping the spoon up the drop-off toward shore. The walleye lay stacked like cordwood right along the edge of the drop-off, near bottom, and I'd feel a jarring strike on almost every cast. The slower the retrieve the better the walleye liked it. I'd alternate and give a pumping jig every six feet or so, and that was when a walleye would climb all over my lure. If a fish was hooked and got off I'd often hook another before I could get my lure to shore.

Another time I was fishing Ontario's famous Moon River for the lunker walleyes the area is noted for. We were fishing out of Wood Bay Lodge near Mac Tier, Ontario. We fished deeper water close to the river mouth. Casting Dardevlets out and letting them sink, we'd have a strike almost every cast. My biggest that day, and my personal record, was a sag-bellied female that scaled 14½ pounds. She struck just like a dead log; the line merely stopped and I couldn't feel a thing. After a couple minutes of jerking on the rod to free my lure I felt it start moving down the river. I tightened into the fish and we had a circus for fifteen minutes before I could slide the fish safely into the meshes.

Trolling, however, is one of the best ways for the fisherman to make the walleye or sauger connection. If the water is shallow I'll troll either a Dardevle, Dardevlet or Cop-E-Cat Imp very slowly along points, drop-offs, sandbars, gravel bars or near any submerged obstruction. A Canadian guide once told me to use any color spoon for walleyes as long as it was yellow. I've followed this advice and it has often resulted in

*Lawrence Richey poses an eleven-pound Dardevle-caught walleye.*

limit catches. I don't know what there is about yellow that is so appealing to a walleye but I've found it's my most productive color for daytime fishing.

If the water is deep I'll rig up a three-way swivel with a twelve-inch dropper to my weight. An eighteen-inch leader down to my lure comprises the rest of the basic rig.

An important factor to consider is that walleyes and sauger are seldom found very far off bottom. If you're going to troll, keep the lure moving very slowly and right down on the floor of the lake. This is where the most fish are found.

Walleyes and sauger are great followers of lures; many times they'll follow and peck gently at a lure for a hundred yards or more before striking hard. One way in which this can be overcome is to apply the lake trout fisherman's "chugging" technique. Slowly raise the rod tip to a vertical position and then drop it rapidly back. The fish will often strike as the lure flutters back toward bottom.

I prefer thinner spoons when trolling since I feel they have an increased wobble and beat that is difficult to find in many other spoons. I like either the Thin Devle or Jr. Flutter Devle. A few fishermen have said they felt I was using too large a lure for walleyes, but if you'll take a look at the toothy maw of a big walleye you'll realize it can easily take a lure of this size into its mouth.

Since walleyes and sauger are often short strikers, sometimes I attach a small split ring to the rear of my treble hooks and insert a long-shank number four single hook. A trick is to add a thin sliver of walleye belly or a white strip of pork rind to the trailer hook. This will usually solve the problem of short strikes and no fish.

Sauger are a little bit different from walleyes in that they'll often hit a lure trolled slightly faster than their cousins would hit. Since sauger seldom average over two pounds I use slightly smaller lures. One of my favorite lures for trolling for these fish is the Devle Dog Jr. in yellow and red chunk with a nickel inside. This lure responds well to a slightly faster troll, although you may have to attach weight in order to get the lure down to the proper level.

Another thing about sauger is that they tend to be more leader-shy than walleyes. I seldom use over six-pound mono for sauger and will troll fifty to seventy-five yards behind the boat. A zigzag trolling pattern that works the lure on and off the drop-offs is a good technique to remember.

One time I was fishing Torch Lake in Michigan's Upper Peninsula near Houghton. It was a gorgeous September day and we met our guide at daybreak. He was anxious to get going, he said, since sauger normally bite best before the sun fully hits the water.

Each of us snapped a Devle Dog Jr. onto his line as we motored down to this hot spot. We eased the lines over and the guide sped down the lake for fifty yards before slowing down. He felt it was best to get the line out quickly so we could begin productive fishing much sooner.

We moved on and off the drop-off for about two hundred yards before my rod tip shot down from the force of a healthy strike. I jabbed the hooks home and felt the power of a strong fish as it surged towards deep water.

My guide shut off the engine and slowly began reeling his line in. The spoon was halfway back to the boat when he had a jarring strike. We jockeyed the fish back and forth before we could land my first sauger—a five-pounder. The other fish weighted slightly less, but our trip was off to a good start.

By nine o'clock that morning we had five lunker sauger on the stringer, and a bulky six-pounder was the largest.

Another method of taking sauger is to cast submerged islands or bars in a river channel. In many locations, like the upper Mississippi River,

*This five-pound sauger is a trophy fish in anybody's book.*

sauger are common along wing dams, and casters often make good catches by working the edges of the river channels or just off submerged islands or rock piles jutting into deep water.

I've anchored on top of rockpiles and cast small Devle Dog Jrs. and Cop-E-Cat Skamps into deep water and slowly retrieved them up the deepwater edge of the rocks. Sauger lie among the rocks and sock a lure presented in this manner.

Hot spots for walleyes are throughout the northern tier of states as well as some unlikely spots such as Arizona. I've had excellent fishing for walleyes in Ontario's Kasagami Lake, Savant Lake, Lake St. Clair (both Michigan and Ontario waters), Lake of the Woods, and Nameigos Lake. Michigan's Burt, Mullet, Cadillac, Mitchell, Houghton, Gogebic, Munuscong and Manistique Lakes are good.

Wisconsin, Minnesota, Ohio (the Lake Erie islands are super), Tennessee, and Kentucky have excellent walleye action.

My best success for sauger has been in Michigan's Torch and Portage Lakes in the Upper Peninsula. Good sauger fishing exists in South Dakota's Oahe Tailwaters and also along the upper Mississippi River in Wisconsin and Minnesota. Some sauger are taken from the Ohio and Tennessee River systems as well as from Minnesota's Lake of the Woods.

These two species are delightful on the table and great fun on the end of a light-action rod. And Dardevle lures are just the ticket for a wealth of fun, fast action and quality eating.

# Thin Spoons Get the Fish

Certain species of freshwater game fish are attracted to the bait-fishlike action of thin metal spoons. The special frantic action these lures produce is conducive to strikes, and Ed Eppinger and the Dardevle crew have several goodies which fall into this category.

The Thindevle, Jr. Flutter Devle, King Flutter Devle and the three sizes of Sagamore spoon each has a wild action which is guaranteed to turn on a schooling and ravenous group of fish such as the coho and chinook salmon, lake trout or even northern pike.

A couple of years ago I was fishing chinook salmon with Capt. Emil

*Lake trout really go after the wild erratic action of the Dardevle thin spoons.*

Dean of Bear Lake, Michigan. We'd wended our way out of the Manistee harbor and into Lake Michigan.

It was September, and chinook were tightly schooled off the Big Manistee river mouth in anticipation of the urge to push upstream to spawn. Emil's fish-locating graph was marking out large numbers of chinook salmon, and boats were tightly grouped together as thousands of lures were pulled through the fish.

Emil has to produce fish for a living and consequently fishes with many different lures. This day we were fishing five downrigger lines and two outriggers, and a different lure went on each. Two downrigger lines were set with Eppinger Dardevle lures; one contained a half-nickle–half-metallic green King Flutter Devle while the other was a chartreuse-with-red-spot 2/0 Sagamore. As we lowered the lures down to the fish Emil said, "Man, look at the action of those spoons." They were bouncing around like marionettes.

We trolled for ten minutes before the rod baited with the King Flutter Devle jerked viciously towards the surface as a big chinook salmon grabbed the spoon. The rod tip was throbbing violently as line melted off the reel.

Emil's mate grabbed the wheel of the *Mary E* and tried to work the boat out of the heavy traffic as I tried to control the bucking rod. I'd just tightened into the fish when the rod strung with the 2/0 Sagamore began banging back and forth in its rodholder as another chinook hurried downlake, the hooks buried in its jaw.

My fish was airborne half the time as I fought to keep it from submarining under a neighboring boat. Emil grabbed the other rod and his fish headed for the stern of the boat and the other downrigger lines. "Speed up! Speed up!" he yelled at the mate. "This fish is going to tangle our lines."

We moved away from Emil's fish just in time to prevent a serious and costly delay. Once a chinook weaves through downrigger lines, the fish is gone and you'll spend nearly an hour getting equipment ready to fish again.

We pressured our fish, and mine was turned twice just before it managed to swim beneath other boats. Emil's fish stayed in the open after that, and within twenty minutes we had the fish nestled safely on ice in the fish box. My King weighed thirty-two pounds while Emil's tipped the scales at thirty-four pounds.

The rest of the day was a repeat of this type of action, although several fish were lost on jumps, to other fishing lines, or simply because they managed to shake the hooks. We ended the day with seven big chinook salmon; Emil's thirty-four-pounder was the largest, but none weighed less than twenty-pounds. The amazing thing about this day's fishing was that all fish were caught on two Dardevle lures, an amazing testimonial to the fish-catching ability of the thin spoons.

Schooling fish like big salmon or lake trout are often triggered into a strike reflex by the wild, violent action of a thin spoon. These lures resemble the bait fish commonly sought by big game fish and their frantic wobble and roll will turn a nonfeeding species into marauding predators. This is especially true whenever the species are making one last feeding spree prior to their spawning runs.

Once I fished Utah's Flaming Gorge Reservoir for brown trout when the fish were near the surface and feeding frantically on bait fish. I trolled and cast several so-called "proven" lures through and around the browns, but nothing happened.

Reaching into my bag of tricks, I pulled out a Jr. Flutter Devle in hammered nickel. I snapped it onto my line and began trolling a faster than normal pattern near the browns. Within minutes my rod jerked toward the lake's surface as a big brown catapulted from the water, his head and gills shaking angrily, before smashing back in a shower of spray.

The brown headed off the bank and dove for bottom with my spinning reel howling as the line peeled off. I quickly reeled in my other line and backed up my Lund boat and Evinrude outboard until I hovered over the fish; my line was as taut as a bowstring. The faint wind whistling through Horseshoe Canyon made an eerie sound as we fought it out.

When the giant brown finally couldn't take the pressure any longer, he

*A thin spoon like the Jr. Flutter Devle accounted for this big brown trout for Randy Colvin.*

*Chunky brown trout like thin spoons since they closely match the action and color of bait fish.*

rolled ponderously to the surface like a large hog and raged back and forth in the line. With that he'd fought his heart out, and I gently led him to the net. He later weighed 18½ pounds on a scale in nearby Manila. Two other trophies fell that day to the magic of the Jr. Flutter Devle.

One thing many people do not realize about the thin spoons, and especially the Sagamores, is they must troll just a little faster to bring out the special fish-attracting action of the lure. Slow speeds simply won't do justice to these spoons.

I've found that when trolling an occasional jerking motion will increase the effectiveness of thin spoons. If I'm hand-holding the rod, without the aid of a rodholder, intermittent jerks on the rod tip will cause these spoons to dart and weave like a punch-drunk prizefighter training for his next bout. This slashing, twisting action greatly simulates the natural action of a bait fish trying to get away from a predator and will trigger a strike from nearby fish.

If I'm fishing thin spoons from a moving boat with the rod in a rodholder, I can attain this identical action by alternately giving the boat a short burst of speed and quickly cutting back to the normal trolling speed. Short, quick turns to port or starboard will also accomplish the same effect.

Many fishermen never realize that thin spoons can be cast and do not necessarily have to trolled. Its true that they can be difficult to cast, especially in the case of the wider Sagamores, but I overcome this by adding one or two number four split shot just ahead of the knot. This added weight will not influence the fish-catching ability of the lure; it merely adds a bit more casting weight.

When cast, a thin spoon behaves much like a pitcher's knuckleball as

*George Richey poses with a brown taken by trolling a thin spoon far behind the boat on Wisconsin's side of Lake Michigan.*

it bobs and weaves in the air currents. Pinpoint accuracy is difficult to attain, but once the lure is out in the water the action can easily be brought out by experimenting with line retrieval speeds.

It's also true that many fishermen feel a thin spoon is best fished in a lake; but I've made some good catches of pike, walleyes and smallmouth bass from rivers with the Thindevle and the Jr. Flutter Devle. They are equally at home in moving or still water.

One time I was fishing Wisconsin's Wolf River for walleyes and the standard jigs and "Wolf River rigs" weren't producing. The fish were holding off wing dams and picking up drifting tidbits or live bait fish as they washed downstream from above.

I'm a constant experimenter with lures, and as a trial I tied on a brass Thindevle and cast it quartering upstream past the wing dam. The lure fluttered to bottom and I inched and twitched it through the eddy water near the dam. Suddenly it stopped for an instant before moving toward me again. The action felt strange and I thought I'd picked up some drifting flotsam.

I kept retrieving and the lure kept coming, but it still felt strange. I jerked my rod tip back in an effort to dislodge the material on the hooks when a savage headshake rippled up the line and down through the rod into my arm.

I set the hooks again, and the line sizzled off for midstream as I kept the rod tip high. We tussled back and forth for several minutes before a golden yellow fish rolled to the surface near the boat. It was a jumbo walleye, at least seven pounds, and it had fallen for the enticing action of a Thindevle being worked deep through the river current.

That lure produced several more fish, including a couple of nice 2½-pound smallmouth bass and one 1½-pound crappie that must have mistaken the lure for an easy meal.

Thin spoons aren't the cure-all for everyone's fishing ills, but they rate a place in any angler's tackle box. They have a seductive wiggle that turns on almost any freshwater or saltwater game fish and they should be used whenever fishing action slows down with other lures. I consider them one of the secret weapons in my tackle box.

# Water Temperature

I've often returned to a crowded dock with a bulging stringer of fish only to be asked the inevitable question: "How did you make such a large catch?" Questioners often immediately relate their sad tale of woe about poor weather, fish not biting, and so on. It's a sad scene that happens all too often across North America.

Anglers should be advised that large catches of fish result more from

*This fisherman takes the water temperature with an electronic water thermometer.*

skill than luck. It's possible, however, to add a smidgen of luck to one's fishing by selecting two of my special weapons—a tackle box full of Dardevles in assorted sizes and colors and an electronic water thermometer. This double-barreled combination is a dual threat to game fish.

I've spent countless years researching fish habits and their water temperature preferences, and whenever I go fishing I always carry along a thermometer to record the temperature of the lake or river. Temperature will often pinpoint exactly where fish should be found. I've been using a Garcia OTP (Oxygen Temperature Probe) model for several years, and it does an excellent job of pinpointing the precise level where fish should be found.

The following temperature preferences for commonly sought game fish prevail across North America but are governed by the locale, water turbidity, water, oxygen content, barometric pressure, wind direction, season of the year and other factors. They should serve solely as a guide to the approximate water temperature preferred by most species.

| *Species* | *Temperature (degrees Fahrenheit)* |
| --- | --- |
| Bluegill and Sunfish | 72 |
| Yellow Perch | 68 |
| Crappies | 68 |
| Walleye and Sauger | 60 |
| Northern Pike and Muskellunge | 65 |
| Coho and Chinook Salmon | 54 |
| Largemouth Bass | 70–72 |
| Smallmouth Bass | 65 |
| Lake Trout and Splake | 59 |
| Rainbow Trout | 60 |
| Brown Trout | 60 |
| Brook Trout | 58 |

The fisherman must learn to combine proper water temperature with habitat requirements or proper bottom conditions for the species of fish he desires to catch. Many books contain this basic knowledge, including this one.

A key to successful fishing is knowing which species of fish is most commonly found in which habitat. Once you can locate productive-looking habitat, and if the water temperature is within a few degrees of the desirable range indicated above, you're on the way to bigger and better catches.

The way an expert fisherman should operate, on brown trout in an inland lake, for instance, would be to know that browns prefer a water temperature of 60° F. He should also know that browns are often found near bottom, off a steep drop-off, near a large point extending far into the lake, along submerged shelves (drop-offs) in deeper water, or occasionally along the deepwater edge of a weed bed along a stretch of hard bottom.

The pro finds an area such as this, anchors his boat, and methodically takes the lake's temperature. He checks the temperature every five feet until he locates the magic point where a brown's metabolism operates at peak efficiency.

Note the depth of the water where you find the proper temperature. It's usually pretty much the same over an entire lake unless a strong wind is blowing. I'd recommend checking the water temperature three or four times a day.

*Steelhead, like this Dardevle-caught fish, are very sensitive to changes in water temperature.*

Once a proper depth and water temperature are found, it is a simple matter to troll, cast, or jig Dardevles in the proper depth where suitable habitat is found.

Certain fish, such as the walleye or largemouth bass, are sensitive to light conditions, and these fish will normally frequent an area where light penetration isn't strong. I often check the dark side of a drop-off, stickup, or river channel for these fish.

One time, in Texas's Sam Rayburn Reservoir, the weather was extremely hot. The sun scorched down at 95 degrees for a week, and most largemouth bass were inactive. I checked a contour map of the lake and found a small pocket, near a creek mouth, where the water was about ten feet deeper than in the surrounding lake.

I checked it out one day with my OTP and found the water was a refreshing 69 degrees. The rest of the lake was sweltering under water registering almost 80 degrees.

I eased back away from the pocket, allowing any bass I may have spooked to return to the area, and then began casting a copper-backed Crackle Frog Weedless Dardevlet into the stickups. I let the spoon settle in a wobbling manner on a tight line, reeled softly to bring out a tiny bit of action, and raised the rod tip to ease the lure over a stickup. Something tried to wrench the rod from my hands.

A bucket-mouthed largemouth surged up through the drowned timber, made a barrel-rolling half jump, foamed back into the water, and submarined for bottom. I leaned hard into my baitcasting rod and cranked the drag down another notch. For several moments it was a standoff as to who was going to give first, I or the fish.

The unrelenting bend in the rod sapped some of the fish's strength; and he rolled to the surface again, came half out of the water, and rattled his head and gill covers at me like a giant tarpon. He tried to surge toward bottom again; but I held tightly, got him skidding across the surface, and slowly worked him into more open water. There we tussled back and forth for five minutes before I could reach down and lip the nine-pounder into the boat.

I'd fish the pocket, hook and either land or lose a bass, move away for an hour, and come back for another try. During one day I managed to boat five largemouth, and the smallest fish from that ten-by-twenty-foot hole of cool water was a seven-pounder. The largest, a sow with a heavily distended stomach, weighed a fraction over ten pounds.

It takes a special knowledge to decide which Dardevle to use after you have considered water temperature and habitat preference for any species of fish. For instance, it would be foolhardy to fish for trophy northern pike with a Dardevlet Spinnie when a regular-sized Dardevle, Troll Devle, Dardevlet or Huskie Devle would work better. At the other extreme, fishing for bluegills or perch would be useless with a large-sized Dardevle when a Spinnie or Weedless Midget would pay bigger dividends.

Many fish, such as northern pike, muskellunge, crappies, and largemouth bass, frequent areas where a weedless Dardevle is often a better choice than the more traditional Dardevle without weedless hooks.

Whenever I find myself in this type of situation after checking the water temperature, I usually resort to a Dardevle Weedless, Dardevlet Weedless or Dardevle Weedless Imp. These lures are designed to snake through tangles of brush, heavy weedbeds, hyacinth patches and through stickups or tangles of treetops.

The temperature-conscious fisherman needs to carry a wide assortment of Dardevles in a variety of colors to take advantage of his knowledge of fish know-how, a tackle box brimming with Dardevles, and a smattering of technique, a fisherman can go almost anywhere and be certain of catching his share of gamefish.

## *What Color Lure?*

One of the most frequently overlooked factors in fishing, regardless of species, is lure color. Many factors enter into a fisherman's choice of lure color: the water conditions, the depth he'll be fishing, and light intensity.

A good fishing buddy of mine, Stan Lievense, formerly a fisheries biologist for the Michigan Department of Natural Resources, and now with the Michigan Department of Commerce-Travel Bureau, has made exhaustive studies of lure color and has consented to share his wisdom with fellow fishermen.

One of the first factors an angler should consider is color penetration in the water. Sunlight is a composite of all the colors of the spectrum. When light penetrates water, its colors filter out in varying degrees. Most species of fish have fairly good color perception and can distinguish intensities and variations.

Studies have shown that in many clear-water lakes, approximately 99 percent of the light is filtered out in the first twenty-five to thirty feet of depth. Water absorbs the radiant energy of light and causes certain colors to filter out as the depth increases. The deeper the water, the more light is absorbed and the darker the lure color appears.

Red is the first color to be filtered out by water. Red lures are generally good during the middle of the day at depths of fifteen feet or less. Early morning or late afternoon, when the sun's rays reach the water's surface at an angle, are not the best times to use a red lure. Reserve red for midmorning to midafternoon, when the sun is high.

Under ideal conditions, orange is a good color for lures down to about forty-five feet. Below that depth, the color fades fast and becomes almost black.

Yellow lures are a favorite choice among fisherman and for good reason. This color shows up well at depths up to eighty feet, and most fishermen seldom fish deeper than this unless they are engaged in deepwater trolling for lake trout or salmon.

Greens and blues are at the other end of the light spectrum, and both colors show up well to 100 feet, with blue getting the edge in depths over 100 feet. White, silver (chrome) and blue are my favorite choices for lure colors when I'm dredging for lake trout or salmon at depths of over 100 feet.

Early morning or late afternoon sun rays which strike the water at a thirty-degree angle or less are almost entirely reflected when the surface water is calm. A ripple or wavy surface will catch some of the low angle rays and illuminate the water, making lure colors more appealing to fish. Maximum underwater illumination occurs at midday when the sun reaches its highest angle.

Direct sun rays are not the sole underwater light source. Underwater scenes are also illuminated to a minor degree by diffused sky light. This source of illumination becomes more important when there is a light cloud cover or whenever it is hazy.

Early in the morning, when the sun's rays are at a low angle and there is very little light penetration, the first color to show in surface waters is blue. As the lighting conditions increase, green begins to penetrate, with blue rays going deeper. As the angle of the sun rises, yellow, orange or red lures will show up best. As the day wears on and the sun sinks lower in the western sky, the depth of color penetration changes in reverse order.

Ultraviolet rays cannot be seen by man or fish, but they convert fluorescent color pigments into light rays. During good light conditions, a fluorescent red lure can be seen as red much deeper than a normal red lure.

White lures gather light rays and present the light in a diffused manner. Black is the absence of all colors and is advisable for maximum contrast.

One time I was trolling for coho salmon off Manistee, Michigan, in the depths of Lake Michigan. The schools of salmon had been pounded for days on end by sport fishermen and were seemingly turned off by every lure. Out of sheer desperation I snapped a black and white stripe Sagamore Flash with a solid black Koho Fly onto my downrigger. I lowered the cannonball and attractor-fly combination to the level of the schooled-up salmon. Five minutes later I had a thrilling strike from a tailwalking coho. Within an hour I had my limit of five coho, and all were caught on the black attractor and fly. At one time I had two salmon on at once, which made for exciting battle.

When I arrived at the dock, interested fishermen gathered around to see what I'd taken the fish on. They were surprised when I told them that black often produces well for almost any species when they've been constantly pounded by more traditional colors. Black gives the fish something they aren't used to seeing.

Over the years I've learned to experiment with lure colors until I find a combination of presentation, depth, retrieval speed, and color that puts fish in a striking mood.

Interestingly enough, Ed Eppinger has been experimenting with lure colors which have proven highly effective. The half-nickle–half-metallic green has been a deadly producer for me on trout, salmon, arctic char, and lake trout. The flat white-with-red-dots and a nickel back has been exceptional in dredging lake trout from the 100-foot depths on the Great Lakes and on Great Bear Lake in the Northwest Territories.

The crystal Dardevles in silver, bronze, and copper are gems among lures. They contain a unique brilliance and sparkle that attract fish at greater depths than other colors of lures. All these new colors are available in all Dardevles lures and sizes.

Yellow lures are a good choice before orange or red, and this is often my choice when casting a shoreline or relatively shallow water for almost any game fish. If you are fishing in a dirty-water lake, consider the better penetrating blues or greens. If the water has a distinct brownish cast, try yellow or a brass-finished lure.

Largemouth bass often are color-blind to yellow or blue. Red Dardevles have been proven the most productive color for bass. Green seems to be the second best color for response from bass.

Dardevles come in a wide variety of sizes, shapes and colors. A fisherman with some knowledge of light penetration and its affect on colors at various depths is on the right road to catching more fish. Simply couple the right color lure with the right depth and present the Dardevle to the fish in a natural manner, and you'll rapidly become known as a consistent fish producer.

# *How to Hire a Guide*

Fishing guides are a rare breed; it takes someone with an uncommonly large amount of fishing savvy—and love for the sport—to make a good guide. Many people have these attributes, but, understandably, not many can make the grade due to personality conflicts with customers or other problems.

Today's guide is a knowledgeable person, in tune with the times, with fishing techniques, and with the particular species of fish he's most adept at catching. Seriously, without some degree of business sense and a knack for handling clients, the average guide will go belly-up within a year.

Good guides are in great demand wherever they are found. I've used the same guides on repeat trips to the subarctic and found them just as affable and eager to please on return visits as on my first encounter. These guides are generally the best fishermen, know the waters well, and know which lure to use and when.

Since good guides are eagerly sought after by fishermen, it often takes either a booking agent or someone in-the-know to secure these guides for a newcomer. I've dealt on and off with booking agents and have found them particularly well suited to cope with guides, customers, and fishing conditions in their area. One of the finest I've seen is Michigan Outdoor Adventures (6767 Miller Rd., Buckley, Michigan 49620). This outfit caters to steelhead, brown trout, coho, and chinook salmon fishermen, and they produce fish for clients when other guides are going empty-handed.

It takes advance planning to pull off a successful fishing trip whether you are fishing in the States or from some far-flung outpost camp in Canada. Planning should involve early initial contact with a suitable guide, checking a list of references he provides, and discussing the area to be fished, the best time to fish there, and other pertinent information.

*Many guides are fishermen and this man is no different when taking out clients. He fishes right along with them and recommends which Dardevle to use for which conditions.*

A year of advance planning is sometimes necessary in order to have a productive trip. Many guides are booked up from year to year by past clients who are satisfied with their services. Some fishermen believe the best policy is to move into the fishing area and then try to enlist the services of a guide, but this is usually ill-fated thinking since most guides are booked on a full-time basis. The only thing you'll find that way is some turkey who *says* he's a good guide. You've got no way to either prove or disprove his claims to fame. If he turns out to be good, you've found the proverbial diamond in a coal pile. What usually happens is, the guide turns out to be a drunk who steals your toasting whiskey, sleeps on the job, knows less about fishing than you do, and couldn't care less whether you catch fish or go home empty-handed. This type of guide should be avoided like an epidemic of smallpox.

Many state and provincial departments of tourism have lists of reliable guides in their area. A letter of inquiry to the state capital or county seat will often turn up the first clue to guides in that region.

The next step is to contact several of these guides and inquire as to their availability to guide during the period in question. Always ask for a list of references and try to acquire names from various parts of the country to eliminate any chance of the guide's naming his "Uncle Harry" as a character reference. This type of biased reference is of little value to a fisherman seeking a guide.

Try to acquire names of customers Joe Guide has handled who have caught less than a limit of fish. If these customers give a glowing account of the guide even though they didn't catch the limit, it will indicate to you that he is expert, reliable and personable.

I've always had my best success by calling past customers on the phone. It takes less time for them to give you a good or bad word than it does for them to write a letter. If you write letters to past customers, always enclose a stamped, self-addressed envelope for their reply. This is just a common courtesy since the other person doesn't owe you the favor of answering an unsolicited letter.

Many guides are booked most of the time, and a common peeve among guides is those customers who call and ask for a fishing date a week away. Too often the guide is booked heavily and the only chance he has of taking on new customers is when a cancellation occurs.

If a customer wishes to book weeks or months in advance there is a chance the guide can work him into a busy schedule. If not, many times the guide himself can recommend someone else that is competent. Many guides trade favors back and forth, and the customer can benefit from this.

Most guides specialize in one type of fishing. It does little good, for either guide or customer, if a client comes expecting to fish in a manner much different from one the guide is used to using. Query ahead as to how fishing is done with this particular individual. If the guide replies in a manner different from the way you wish to fish, then look to another source.

Many guides, and many fishermen, are temperamental; they demand understanding and respect of their wishes. I've guided for years, and if there is anything I can't stand it's to have a customer hire me and then tell me how he wants to fish. I always explain to my clients exactly how fishing will be done. If, at that time, they wish not to fish, no one is hurt by the decision.

Some guides are leathery, foul-mouthed people, used to fishing with men only. Some will not guide women or a husband-wife team. If you like to cuss like a mule skinner, and the guide thinks it's awful, you'll have a miserable day. On the other hand, if the guide blurts out every vulgar word you've ever heard of, and some you haven't, this likely will rub you (or anyone with good taste) the wrong way.

I've known guides that absolutely refuse to believe anyone knows as much about fishing as they do. I once knew a guide that would smack his customers' hands if they touched the drag on the spinning or baitcasting reels. Odd treatment like this doesn't endear a guide to a sport paying good money for a quality outdoor recreational experience. Letters to the guide, or better, a phone call, will help determine the character's likes and dislikes among fishermen.

I'm often asked what a guide should be paid. I've got a deep gut feeling on this; I feel the best guides are never paid enough and the poor guides aren't worth whatever money they receive. I've paid as little as fifteen dollars a day for Indian guides in Canada and as much as a hundred dollars for a good guide in Michigan. The average falls somewhere in between, but I'd say that roughly seventy to ninety dollars per day for two fishermen isn't unreasonable. Additional customers over two normally calls for an increase in pay.

When you've agreed on the guide's charge for a day of his time, just remember that you're buying his time and knowledge, not a limit catch of fish, or even one fish. Every guide has off days where the fish simply won't cooperate and no one can be blamed.

Another thing you aren't buying is a packhorse for transporting all your worthless equipment. Guides are human beings and subject to the same type of treatment you'd expect. I've seen some timid guides lugging 150 pounds of tackle boxes, rods and reels, and assorted junk for clients that snicker about "getting their money's worth." Such thinking is unfair and cruel. I've often told customers to leave their junk in the car and use my equipment. I always refuse to be treated like a servant, and most guides feel the same.

This brings up the subject of what a guide should furnish and what the customer should bring. In remote sections of Canada where fishing tackle is at a premium, most guides believe the customer should furnish his own gear.

Yet in locales where tackle is easily available, many guides believe the customer is much better off leaving his own equipment home unless he absolutely insists on using it. Many guides in these places would prefer that the customer use their equipment since it is proven for the species of fish they are going after. Local lures and methods of fishing are part of the reason why anyone hires a guide, and a good guide will know what to use, when to use it, and why. A customer with a tackle box full of junk lures simply won't have the needed tackle to insure a good day on the water.

A customer should always listen to the advice of a guide. These people have learned, over the years, how to fish in their area, and this is what you are paying hard-earned bucks to learn. I always try to pick the brain of a guide in order to learn as much as possible in a given amount of time. Most guides are frank, open talkers once you impress upon them that you're interested in learning.

I have run into problems with Indian guides in Canada when I've been after trophy fish. They feel most fishermen simply want to catch as many fish as possible. I've had several minor arguments with Indian guides until I've convinced them that I'm after trophy fish, not just the average run-of-the mill pan stinkers.

If you've got a problem like this, talk it over as calmly as possible with the guide to insure he doesn't have sore feelings over the encounter. But make it clear, preferably in advance, just what you wish to catch.

If it's trophies, say so. If you just want fish, then that's another matter. A good guide must be receptive to the wishes of his client, within reason.

Another bone of contention is the length of days and meals. In some areas a guide will furnish the noon meal as a matter of course, while in others the guide expects to be fed by the client. This must be settled ahead of time, because if the client goes fishing expecting to be fed by the guide, he may go hungry while the guide wolfs down a brown-bag lunch.

A guide's day varies from one locale to another. For some, it's a banker's day of nine to five. Other guides work from sunup to sundown and call it a day's fishing. Some area guides take a midday break of two hours for a nap and meal during the hottest part of the day. If you feel this unreasonable, either obtain another guide or offer him more money for his time. Guides are in business to make money and few would refuse a chance to pick up some extra bucks.

A guide is an important asset only if he is good. I've found that tipping the guide a ten or twenty-dollar bill increases your chance of hiring him again in the future. I feel a tip is in order if a guide performs his duties well, is well mannered, and has your best interests at heart. I don't feel

*Most guides double as shoreline cooks and Charley Hamelin, guide for Bransons Lodge on Great Bear Lake, is both a good cook and a good guide.*

the customer should tip if the guide is slack in his duties, is rude and arrogant, or furnishes faulty equipment for your use.

Tipping isn't contingent upon a limit catch of fish. I've tipped guides when I've been skunked simply because they have done everything possible to insure my having a good fishing trip. Whether you catch fish should not be the sole criterion for offering a guide a tip.

Guides are a necessary part of the fishing picture, and a good one's friendship should be cultivated. I've always held that if you treat a guide like you'd wish to be treated, he'll do everything in his power to provide you with a good fishing trip.

## Arctic Char and Grayling

Two species of fish remain so distantly removed from most fishermen that they only dream of catching them. The arctic char and arctic grayling are fish that dreams are made of; the fisherman easily conjures up thoughts of fast—racehorse fast—streams where the midnight sun shines for almost twenty-four hours, where sleek red-sided char, fresh from the Arctic Ocean, race upstream on late summer spawning runs, or thoughts of swift rivers and remote, spruce-rimmed lakes where dimpled rises or underwater swirls mark the passage of the arctic grayling.

Strangely enough, these fish aren't difficult to catch; the biggest problem is to scrape together enough cash to spring for such a trip which will involve floatplane travel, prospecting for good numbers of fish to catch, and having enough Dardevles of various sizes to cope with any fishing situation.

In 1977, for instance, my wife and I boarded an Air Canada flight from Chicago to Edmonton, Alberta. We spent the night in the lovely Chateau Lacombe and winged our way north to Great Bear Lake in a huge Siddeley Hawker. The flight was uneventful except for a brief layover in Yellowknife; then we proceeded to Sawmill Bay on Great Bear Lake.

The pilot for Bransons Lodge picked us up, and fifteen minutes later we were greeted by Ernie Dolinsky and his charming wife Mavis. As owners-operators of Bransons Lodge, they bend over backwards to show guests the best possible fishing. Although Great Bear is world-famous for its huge lake trout, Kay and I were interested in both arctic char and grayling.

We spent several days sampling the trout-rich waters nearby for grayling and took quite a few fish of three pounds or better. Ernie then said, "Would you like to try Dismal Lake? It's a short flight from here and the grayling are huge!'' We jumped at the chance like hatchery trout to a liver pellet.

We spent two days doing battle with trophy grayling in Dismal and found that small Dardevle Midgets, Lil Devles, and Dardevle Spinnies were just the ticket when cast into the shallows among the rocks and fallen trees and retrieved slowly. The best finishes seemed to be all nickel, brass or copper, although we did catch a few grayling on the yellow with five red diamonds.

The total cost for eight days of delightful fishing at Bransons was about $1,300 each from Edmonton, Alberta.

Grayling rove lakes and rivers in fairly large schools. I've seen pods of grayling, working the shallows of Great Bear and Dismal Lakes, that would number from twenty to forty fish. The average size was about 1½ pounds, although good numbers of three-pounders are present and the world record, a five-pound fish, was caught by Jeanne Branson, former owner of Bransons lodge, on Great Bear. Fish of this size are not common anywhere.

Both male and female grayling possess a distinctively colored dorsal

*Greg Meadows admires a chunky arctic grayling which struck a small Dardevle near Bransons Lodge on Great Bear Lake.*

fin, the male's being proportionately larger than the female's. This dorsal fin bears irregular but distinct rows of dark spots and is often tinged with white or pink along the upper edge. This brightly colored fin is the grayling's drawing card. Fishermen the world over love a fish that is attractive or distinctive, and the grayling certainly falls in this class. The dorsal fin on a grayling male is low in the front and sweeps high toward the rear; the female's dorsal fin is just the opposite.

Catching grayling usually isn't a problem; the biggest factor involved is finding good concentrations of the fish. Some of the nicest fish come from swift rivers where larger numbers of grayling are found holding at the edge of fast water behind a huge boulder.

I've fished several unnamed streams in the Northwest Territories and the Yukon where grayling actually compete for a well-placed lure or spinner. I once fished the Katseyedie River in the Northwest Territories where grayling, their sail-like banners held majestically upright, fought the bend of the rod until they were subdued. These fish customarily were in the three-to-four-pound class, and a silver 1/8 ounce Notangle Spinner was the key to angling success.

I'd cast just above the great boulders and allow the spinner to drift down into the pocket of dead water. A grayling would dart from behind the rock and grab the dainty lure. It always took some doing to coax the fish from the fast water into a calm eddy where it could be lifted from the water, unhooked and released.

Spinning gear is the ticket for big grayling. Like the wary brown trout, a grayling is often a bit leader-shy. I never use over six-pound mono in a river, although you often run the hazard of hooking a large northern pike, which may saw through the fine line. When I fish a grayling lake I'll ordinarily use four-pound mono and take my time with the fish.

Small spinners, like the Notangle, are exceptional lures for grayling in lakes or rivers. Since they have small mouths, it's best to use small lures. I've used both the plain hook and squirrel-tail Notangle spinners in 1/8 ounce. Silver generally produces well, although I've also had good success with brass, copper, or red and white. Generally, the plain hook outproduces the squirrel-tail model.

Occasionally I'll remove the treble hook from a Notangle Spinner and replace it with a single long-shank number-twelve hook. It is very important to keep the hook and lure size small for grayling. They have dainty mouths and cannot accept a lure if it's too large.

The sail-finned arctic grayling is found from Alaska east through the Yukon and Northwest Territories, northern Saskatchewan, northern Alberta and in certain sections of northern British Columbia.

Some excellent fishing can be found in Alaska's Nation and Holtina Rivers; in the Northwest Territories' Great Bear, Great Slave, Dismal, and Colville lakes, and below White Eagle Falls on the Camsell River; in Saskatchewan's Athabasca and Reindeer lakes; in the Yukon's Rancheria and Swift rivers and countless lakes; and in Alberta's Athabasca and Peace Rivers and their tributaries as well as portions of the McLeod River, Christmas Creek, Trout Creek and Kinky Lake.

The arctic char is one of the most highly prized game fish available to fishermen. It attains great size, and the male is vividly beautiful in his spawning colors. The wild areas where these fish are found have to be some of the most breathtaking country in the northern hemisphere.

One of the major characteristics with which char endear themselves to anglers is their willingness to strike spoons. Char, fresh from salt water, whether it be along the Arctic Ocean or in Quebec's Ungava Bay region, feed heavily on capelin, sand eels and sculpins. They are used to feeding on flashing bait fish in open water, and this characteristic is carried over when the fish begin their spawning runs off river mouths and into the rivers themselves.

It's when char arrive in milling hordes off river mouths in anticipation of their spawning run that anglers travel the full length of the North American continent to lock horns with this gamy species. Char often weigh up to and over twenty pounds in their western range, which would include Alaska, the Northwest Territores, Victoria Island, and the off-shore waters of the Yukon.

Char taken from northern Quebec in the Ungava Bay region, northern Labrador, Baffin Island, Iceland, Greenland, and in a few scattered locations along the northeastern shore of Hudson Bay are, as a rule, smaller fish. A char of fifteen pounds is a trophy from northeastern waters, and the average would be closer to ten pounds. Furthermore, very few char with the brilliant red or carmine sides are taken from the eastern waters.

Most of the gorgeous male char with flaming flanks are taken from a few rivers east of Coppermine, Northwest Territories. Bransons Lodge has an exclusive lease on an unnamed river east of Coppermine where char grow large and many have blood red sides; such fish are the goal of most sportsmen seeking a trophy to mount.

It's when char enter their spawning streams that some excellent fishing occurs. One time I was fishing the Tunulik River, east of Fort Chimo, Quebec, when the char were packed into small pockets of rushing water and they would often follow a red-with-white-stripe Rok't-Devlet for twenty feet through the raging torrent before striking.

*The author gills a silvery arctic char from northern Quebec's Tunulik River. It struck a yellow-with-five-red-diamonds Dardevle.*

*A hefty silvery char is netted after a powerful struggle on Ungava Bay.*

On the strike, a fish would charge off on an initial panicky dash for about one hundred feet, throw itself into the air in a cartwheeling jump, land amid the haystacking rapids, and tear off downstream. I caught more than twenty char one day on various Dardevles, and each fish took me down almost to a bare spool and required anywhere from fifteen to thirty minutes to land. Most hauled me at least a quarter mile down the river.

Polarized sunglasses were required to spot resting char in pockets of eddy water created by the swirling currents washing around huge boulders or ledges of multicolored rocks.

At first glance the fish would appear motionless on bottom, but occasionally you'd spot the sweeping flick of a tail as the fish held its position against the current. Spotcasting with quick sinking Rok't Devlets, Dardevles, Dardevlets, Seadevlets and Seadevle Imps was necessary to produce jarring strikes. My most productive colors for river fishing have been nickel inside with red and white stripe, yellow with five red diamonds, and the Orange Potato Bug with brass inside.

Many rivers are so swift that the addition of a split shot or two immediately above the lure is required to aid in sinking it to the level of the resting char.

An erratic retrieve has proven best for me. I'll usually cast it slightly upstream from the fish, allow it to sink, and begin bringing it back in a stop-start, jerk-pause type of retrieve.

Since most char fishing is done in rivers with huge rock formations, it becomes necessary to touch up hook points periodically with a hone or file. Many strikes are missed simply because the angler forgets this very important detail. Keep those hook points sharp!

Openwater fishing, although not as spectacular as angling in a wild, whitewater river, is often more productive than fishing where the force of the river's current enables many a char to get away.

The key to openwater fishing, whether it's Ungava Bay or offshore from Coppermine, is selecting an area where char are found. Tides fluctuate in these northern areas, and as the tides change, char move into the river mouths or near offshore islands to feed.

Look for areas where a distinct current is formed by the tide rushing between two islands or around the tip of an island. Char are often found in quieter eddy water on the inside or outside of these strong currents.

I like a quick-sinking lure with lots of flash, so on my trips to the subarctic for char I always take along a large supply of various-sized Dardevles to match any water or river condition. For open water I prefer Dardevles, Dardevlets, Rok't Devlets and Cop-E-Cat Jrs. The latter lure

*Casting to arctic char in a raging whitewater river is grand sport with Dardevles.*

*These fishermen admire a char taken on a chartreuse-with-red-spot Dardevle.*

works extremely well when casting off islands and river mouths, because the size and shape closely imitate the char's forage fish. I like nickel, hammered nickel, hammered nickel with blue, nickel inside with red and white stripe, and chartreuse with red spots and a nickel inside. I'm not sure why the chartreuse coloration works, but I managed a limit catch in a half hour off the mouth of the Coppermine River with this color.

Prospecting for cruising char in open water involves trying different areas and depths until you locate a school of fish. When you do, the action is immediate and fast-paced. I've found that a normal retrieve that brings out the seductive throb of the lure is best under most circumstances, although you should experiment with sinking time in order to bring the lure through the proper level.

An alternate retrieve that worked one time for me among the offshore islands in Ungava Bay, near the mouth of the Tunulik River, was to cast out, allow the lure to settle for about five seconds, and then bring it back with a rapid retrieve for about ten feet. This stop-and-go, with brief pauses to allow the lure to sink, absolutely drove the char wild.

Char customarily take lures quite deep, and many times a treble hook isn't necessary if you intend to release fish. I often pinch down the barbs on treble hooks or replace the treble with a single salmon hook. This facilitates the ultimate safe release of unwanted char.

Ungava Bay in northern Quebec remains a relatively untouched area for char fishermen. Good fishing exists in or near the Koksoak, Tunulik, Whale and George rivers as well as in Ungava Bay itself.

Fishermen commuting to the Northwest Territories can find excellent char fishing in or near the Coppermine and Tree rivers as well as in countless unnamed and seldom-fished streams flowing into Coronation Gulf, Bathurst Inlet, and Victoria Island.

The arctic char and grayling are two of North America's most treasured game fish. You'll expend time, money and much energy getting to areas where these fish are found, but it will result in a trip you'll long remember.

# *Dardevle Ice Fishing Techniques*

Ice had formed a twelve-inch mantle over Michigan's Keweenaw Bay. Ice shanties dotted the bay and anglers scurried to and from shore, the majority of them leaving empty-handed except for their gear.

As we walked onto the ice I stopped several fishermen and asked if they'd had any luck with trout. The answer was unanimous; no one had hooked a fish although several reported seeing quite a number of browns, steelhead, and lake trout ease past their hole.

A local fisherman had made his shanty available to us. It was the first time I'd fished Keweenaw Bay and only the second for my friend.

We eased the door of the light-proof shanty closed, and a whole new world was revealed to us. The water took on a luminous glow, and within minutes I spotted a steelhead cruising ten feet below the ice.

Winter trout and most other species hemmed in by ice are usually on the feed. Trout, in particular, cruise back and forth off river mouths looking for something to eat. The six-pound steelhead was no exception. He was hungry, but wouldn't strike just anything; he wanted something to chomp on that looked like a bait fish.

I lowered a silver and blue Devle Dog Jr. into the hole and spooled it to the ten-foot level. I jigged it vertically three or four times in short, three-inch lifts, allowed it to remain motionless for two or three seconds, and then gave it another short jig. A steelhead darted in from one side, grabbed the spoon in his jaws, and headed for deeper water. I jabbed the short jigging rod upwards to set the hook and then sat frozen to my chair as the steelhead peeled twenty-five yards of line off my baitcasting reel.

The steelie then headed for bottom in a power dive that had my rod tip jerking down into the ice hole. The fish stopped and I began leaning on him. He reversed his field, headed for the surface like he was going to bust his own hole in the ice, and then turned and swam under my ice hole while my hands cranked furiously on the reel in an attempt to catch up.

A few minutes later I led the exhausted fish up to the ice hole. He came, in a rolling manner, like a silvery corkscrew twisting through the water. As he bobbed to the surface of the shanty hole, my partner slipped a small gaff under his chin and hoisted him into the shanty.

A half hour later a lake trout cruised by, just off bottom. My buddy lowered his chartreuse-with-red-spot Devle Dog down to the fish, jigged it up and down with sharp, two-foot lifts, and was amazed to see the laker swim up and inhale the lure in a fluid motion. We were then treated to a thrilling display of power as the trout stirred up the lake mud with broad sweeps of his tail in an effort to rid himself of the lure buried in his jaw.

Ten minutes later the laker came up from the depths with the strange luminescence common to lakers surfacing from deep water. The fish rolled several times in the line, and its pearly glow could be seen in twenty feet of water. I did the honors this time, and we soon had two nice trout lying on the ice outside the shanty.

Trout of all species are suckers for a properly jigged Dardevle. If the

*This angler lands a nice trout through the ice while another person fishes in the background. He caught his fish while jigging Jr. Devle Dogs.*

lure is jigged in a manner which represents a wounded minnow, or something else good to eat, any trout in the area will come to check out a possible meal.

Jigging from a light-proof shanty is often more productive than simply jigging from open ice. From a shanty it's often possible to spot a trout cruising and to present the lure to him at his level. And if you can see the fish you can possibly determine which type of jigging tactic interests him.

Another time I was jigging at Copper Harbor, Michigan, for splake—a cross between brook and lake trout. The fish were hungry, no doubt about it. But they were also skeptical about striking jigged lures. We finally determined we were using too large a lure with our Devle Dog Jrs. and switched to a smaller Lil Devle in silver and blue. The smaller lure interested the fish, but still they held back about three feet and watched as we jigged the lure constantly in an up-and-down manner.

Finally I decided to simply twitch the tiny spoon an inch or two and

*Richard Smith poses with a fat, three-pound splake taken by jigging.*

give it a brief, one-second pause between twitches. The first time I paused, a three-pound splake zoomed in and struck so daintily that I couldn't feel the take. If I hadn't been watching the fish I'd never have known he had the spoon in his mouth. Once we landed that first fish on the twitch-pause method, we went on to rack up a limit catch of splake.

Bigger trout, such as trophy browns, steelhead, or lake trout, often respond best to a spoon jigged up and down with sharp, two-foot lifts. Lower the rod tip quickly and allow the spoon to flutter back down. Most strikes will occur as the spoon settles.

I've also learned that when jigging through the ice for trout a small sliver of sucker or smelt meat or the tail from one of these fish can be added to the spoon. It slightly affects the balance of a Dardevle, but occasionally it will spell the difference between landing trout and going home empty-handed. The smell of the fish flesh and the glitter of the lure are a deadly combination for winter trout.

Smaller trout require smaller Dardevles, and I've successfully used the Lil Devle, Dardevle Spinnie, Dardevle Midget and Dardevle Skeeter to good advantage. The best colors are blue, nickel on both sides, half nickel and half blue with nickel inside, chartreuse with red spots, and yellow with five red diamonds and brass inside.

Larger trout require a heavier lure, especially in deep water. I've used the Rok't Devlet, Dardevle, and Seadevle Imp in silver, blue, and flat white with red dots and a nickel back. These colors show up well at customary lake trout depths.

Jigging for walleyes and northern pike is great sport in many Michigan, Wisconsin, and Minnesota locations. Larger lures like the Dardevle, Dardevlet and Rok't Devlet can be used along the edges of weed beds, sunken islands, or near a wide river mouth. These spring spawners often congregate off a river mouth during the winter in anticipation of moving upstream to spawn when the ice goes out.

Walleyes are normally taken near bottom during winter months; northern pike are usually found near bottom but often cruise several feet off bottom. Experimentation with jigging depth is needed when fishing for northerns.

A superb ice fishing trick for yellow perch, bluegills and crappies involves using the Dardevle Skeeter and Dardevle Skeeter Plus on light monofilament. I normally use just two-pound test. I locate my ice fishing hole close to a weed bed for bluegills and crappies, and for perch wherever experience dictates. Yellow perch are migratory, here today and gone tomorrow. It often takes several moves to locate schools of perch.

Although I've caught a good many of the bigger 'gills and crappies on bare spoons, quite a few of these fish are attracted to the quiet flashing of the tinest Dardevles. I substitute a long shank number fourteen streamer hook for the tiny treble and then attach a corn borer, wax worm or wiggler to the bare hook. Bluegills and crappies are curious feeders and often come in to the bait for a chance at a free meal.

Small spoons for small fish should be barely jiggled in the water. Too much flash or up-and-down motion will send them scurrying for cover for fear that a predator may be coming after them.

Begin jigging by barely twitching the rod tip upward. Allow the lure to stop shaking, slowly raise it an inch or two, and cautiously impart a shiver to the spoon. Let it rest again for an instant and raise it another inch or two. Keep this up until you've covered all depths from the bottom to the ice. Somewhere in between you'll find the level these fish are using.

Yellow perch are more active feeders, and slightly larger spoons can be used to jig a mess of fine tasty perch onto the ice. Try the Dardevle Midget or the Spinnie for perch and substitute a single number ten long-shank hook for the treble. To this hook I'd suggest adding small shiner minnow, a perch eye or a wiggler. Perch are attracted by the flash of the spoon and the bait provides an added tidbit.

Begin jigging near bottom since perch are often bottom-oriented. If this doesn't produce, work slowly upward a foot at a time until you hit fish. If you work a hole twice from the bottom to the surface and don't get a strike, pick up and move in search of the perch schools.

Perch often respond best to a rapid up-and-down jigging stroke of about six to twelve inches. If this doesn't produce, try jigging in shorter, sharper lifts. Once in a while a long, two-foot lift will bring about a strike. Perch normally strike as the spoon settles back into position.

Another trick the experts use is to jig with two rods in the same hole with a different lure or color on each rod. Silver or chartreuse spoons are good on bright days, while copper or brass often work best on an overcast day.

The winter fisherman needn't stash his Dardevles until spring. All he has to do is try adapting openwater techniques to ice fishing. The results may make a confirmed ice fisherman from someone normally content to laze away winter days in front of the TV set.

# Saltwater Fishing: A Dardevle Natural

Many anglers have the mistaken notion that Dardevle lures are destined for use in fresh water only. This line of thinking has caused them to overlook the unlimited possibilities the lures have to offer in saltwater.

The variety of game fish found in the salt would stagger the imagination of any freshwater fisherman. Nearly any saltwater species you can name—white sea bass, black sea bass, bluefish, striped bass, barracuda, snook, tarpon and so on—can be taken on one of the many varieties of Dardevles.

One of the most enjoyable and (until a big fish is hooked) laziest methods of saltwater fishing is vertical jigging off California for white sea bass, which can run as heavy as seventy pounds. This type of fishing would put to shame almost anything the freshwater fisherman tries. Seadevle, Seadevlet or Seadevle Imps are used. The lure is jigged up and down near the bottom until the spoon stops. Until you set the hook into a supercharged bundle of hyped-up sea bass, you haven't lived. It takes heavy tackle and strong back and arm muscles to work these big fish up from bottom.

Bluefish, those razor-toothed gamesters found along the Atlantic Ocean shore, are especially susceptible to either trolling or casting with the larger Dardevles. One time I was fishing near Florida's Sebastian Inlet. The bluefish lay just off the rip and we couldn't reach them from shore, so we took a boat out and began trolling Seadevlets through the school of ravenous fish.

I wound up and cast my spoon out behind the boat and had just put the rod in a rodholder when the rod tip shot down behind the stern. A ten-pound blue had grabbed the spoon and was headed for home.

I set the hook, although it really didn't need setting, and held on as the

*Nick Karas shows a nice bluefish taken off New York on a Dardevle.*

fish tore the water apart in an attempt to get free. Within several minutes I had it worked close to the boat and watched as other bluefish tried to take the spoon away from the hooked fish.

In a matter of a few action-packed hours we caught twenty-five bluefish and returned all but the few we planned to have for a camp-out dinner that evening. The point behind this anecdote is that Dardevles can spell all the difference in the world between saltwater action and a day on the way. More people should give them a try for the salty species of fish.

Barracuda, that terror of the flats, is another likely candidate for Dardevle fishing, saltwater style. I've taken some hellish 'cudas while casting Seadevles and Huskie Devles in southern waters.

When these fish work in on the flats, or into brackish water back in the mangroves, a well-placed cast across the 'cuda's bow will almost certainly result in a strike. If the water is shallow it pays to stand in the bow and spot the fish before it becomes alerted to the presence of the boat.

Once you've hooked a tailwalking barracuda on light spinning tackle, you'll be hooked on saltwater fishing just as that savage fish is hooked on the end of your line.

A word of caution, though: use a six- or eight-inch wire leader for toothy species like the barracuda. They can make mincemeat of monofilament in an instant.

Casting with the big Seadevles or Troll Devles is one way of catching striped bass when they work into the suds to feed on bait fish. It takes a hefty rod and plenty of backbone to cast these lures and to bring out the action in them, but wading fishermen along the Atlantic are finding good action with both spoons.

Offshore trollers find good action with bluefin tuna, Atlantic bonito and other species when the proper size Dardevle is trolled fairly fast so the lure skips across the surface like a frantic forage fish. It often takes two or three ounces of trolling sinker ahead of the lure to keep it down at a rapid trolling pace, but these lures work wonders.

Dardevles are as suited to saltwater fishing as bacon is to fried eggs. Just select the proper size spoon to closely imitate the bait fish being ravished by game fish and you'll be in business.

## *Exotic Dardevle Trophies*

Many sportsmen feel fishing in North America is the best they'll ever be able to hope for. Thoughts of fishing in Africa or South America are pipe dreams. It's pretty heady stuff to contemplate a far-flung trip to another continent for the sole purpose of catching exotic game fish.

In today's jet-age world, travel to remote hot spots isn't nearly as expensive as a sportsman might think. Braniff International (P. O. Box 35001, Dallas, Texas 75235) is one airline serving sportsmen with a wide variety of vacation trips to South America where they can tangle with dorado, large trout, payara, piranha, peacock bass or any one of a number of larger exotic game fish.

Braniff has a toll-free number so that an interested fisherman can easily find out just how reasonable it is to fly to South America for fast-paced action. Call 1-800-527-2670.

Much of the delight in any fishing trip is advance planning; this form of pre-trip dreaming gives a fine edge to your fishing fever. Regardless of where you are planning to go, it pays to put as much time as possible into making sure you've got the proper equipment for the fishing conditions.

Most flights allow a fisherman forty-four pounds of baggage without additional charges. Whenever I plan a trip my first consideration is for my tackle; clothing can be washed daily if need be, but many fishing camps, especially in South America, have few if any lures to sell if you run out. I'll skimp on my duded-up evening clothes in order to carry more lures, rods and reels, and other extra fishing equipment. If you run short back in the boondocks somewhere and the fish are literally mauling Cop-E-Cats in red and white, and you just lost your last spoon to a savage dorado, it does little good to whine and complain.

Buck Rogers, an outdoor-travel writer friend of mine, makes many

*This pretty young angler shows off two average tiger fish taken from Rhodesia's Kariba Lake on Dardevles.*

trips each year to widely scattered locations in South America to sample the fishing. His advice to fishermen heading south is, "Take ten pounds of spoons (Dardevles)." By following his own advice he's been able to furnish other fishermen with badly needed Dardevles when they've run out.

Dardevles, in sizes slightly larger than those used for most North American fishing, are like gold in South America. Some of the larger tackle shops in the big cities carry a limited supply, but no one back in fishing country handles any quantity of lures. If you fail to bring your own supply, the trip could be in vain.

The Cop-E-Cat is one of the best producing Dardevles in South America. It can be retrieved faster than many other spoons and is very productive for dorado in Paraguay and Uruguay. This golden-colored game fish reaches an average weight of fifteen pounds or more and is known to scale upwards of sixty pounds. It takes a rough, tough spoon and strong hooks to control this battler.

The peacock bass of the Amazon River country is another spectacular fighter that attracts North American fishermen. Again, the Cop-E-Cat in red and white stripe with nickel back is a proven producer for this South American bass, which averages about five pounds and ranges up to twelve pounds. Many of these fish are taken by casting close to the shoreline.

South America doesn't have the patent on all fishing; Africa, too, is currently producing some of the finest fishing in the world.

Some of the hottest angling is for the tooth-studded tiger fish in the Zambezi River or Kariba Lake in Rhodesia. This striped game fish looks like something from prehistoric times. Its mouthful of daggerlike teeth is capable of ripping off an angler's fingers if he is careless enough to get too close.

Much of the tiger fishing is done by trolling in Rhodesia's lakes, and large Dardevles such as the Cop-E-Cat, Huskie Devle, or Seadevle are just right to entice these fish into striking.

It's possible to cast certain portions of Rhodesia's lake shoreline for tiger fish and watch herds of elephants grazing in the background. A myriad of wild birds and animals form a constant parade in front of the fisherman, and this setting in itself is a fantastic advantage of a foreign fishing trip.

Tiger fish will average about eight pounds, but some of the larger specimens will range up to twenty pounds. This is a hard-muscled and ferocious fighting game fish, and the addition of a mounted tiger fish to an angler's trophy room wall is a prize indeed.

Dardevles are an excellent choice for a globe-trotting fisherman. They've taken the above-mentioned species as well as trout and giant northern pike from Ireland, huge catfish from South America, trout by the score from Argentina, Peru and Ecuador, trout and other game fish from Australia and New Zealand, and a wide variety of saltwater gamesters from all the oceans of the world.

The Dardevle line of lures should definitely be included whenever a fisherman plans a trip for any species of fish. When you're after the so-called "oddball" species of game fish, Dardevles should not be overlooked.